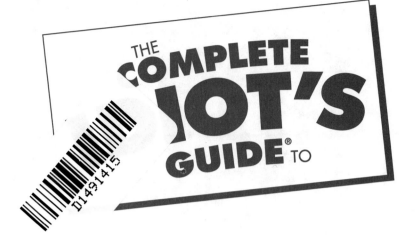

THE
COMPLETE IDIOT'S GUIDE® TO

The World of
Narnia

Kintore College
75 Charles St W
Toronto, ON
Canada
416-944-8323

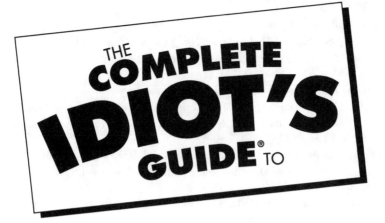

THE **COMPLETE** **IDIOT'S** **GUIDE**® TO

The World of
Narnia

*by James S. Bell Jr. and
Cheryl Dunlop*

ALPHA

A member of Penguin Group (USA) Inc.

ALPHA BOOKS

Published by the Penguin Group

Penguin Group (USA) Inc., 375 Hudson Street, New York, New York 10014, USA

Penguin Group (Canada), 90 Eglinton Avenue East, Suite 700, Toronto, Ontario M4P 2Y3, Canada (a division of Pearson Penguin Canada Inc.)

Penguin Books Ltd., 80 Strand, London WC2R 0RL, England

Penguin Ireland, 25 St. Stephen's Green, Dublin 2, Ireland (a division of Penguin Books Ltd.)

Penguin Group (Australia), 250 Camberwell Road, Camberwell, Victoria 3124, Australia (a division of Pearson Australia Group Pty. Ltd.)

Penguin Books India Pvt. Ltd., 11 Community Centre, Panchsheel Park, New Delhi—110 017, India

Penguin Group (NZ), 67 Apollo Drive, Rosedale, North Shore, Auckland 1311, New Zealand (a division of Pearson New Zealand Ltd.)

Penguin Books (South Africa) (Pty.) Ltd., 24 Sturdee Avenue, Rosebank, Johannesburg 2196, South Africa

Penguin Books Ltd., Registered Offices: 80 Strand, London WC2R 0RL, England

International Standard Book Number: 978-1-59257-617-3
Library of Congress Catalog Card Number: 2007926847

09   08   07   8   7   6   5   4   3   2   1

Interpretation of the printing code: The rightmost number of the first series of numbers is the year of the book's printing; the rightmost number of the second series of numbers is the number of the book's printing. For example, a printing code of 07-1 shows that the first printing occurred in 2007.

Printed in the United States of America

Note: This publication contains the opinions and ideas of its authors. It is intended to provide helpful and informative material on the subject matter covered. It is sold with the understanding that the authors and publisher are not engaged in rendering professional services in the book. If the reader requires personal assistance or advice, a competent professional should be consulted.

The authors and publisher specifically disclaim any responsibility for any liability, loss, or risk, personal or otherwise, which is incurred as a consequence, directly or indirectly, of the use and application of any of the contents of this book.

Most Alpha books are available at special quantity discounts for bulk purchases for sales promotions, premiums, fund-raising, or educational use. Special books, or book excerpts, can also be created to fit specific needs.

For details, write: Special Markets, Alpha Books, 375 Hudson Street, New York, NY 10014.

Publisher: *Marie Butler-Knight*
Editorial Director: *Mike Sanders*
Managing Editor: *Billy Fields*
Acquisitions Editor: *Michele Wells*
Development Editor: *Julie Bess*
Production Editor: *Kayla Dugger*

Copy Editor: *Krista Hansing Editorial Services, Inc.*
Cartoonist: *Brigit Bell Ritchie*
Cover/Book Designer: *William Thomas*
Indexer: *Johnna Vanhoose Dinse*
Layout: *Brian Massey*
Proofreader: *Aaron Black*

To my three lovely daughters, for making Narnia a father/daughter thing over the last 22 years: Rosheen, who read them in record time; Brigit, who used them as a launching pad to become a voracious reader; and Caitlin, who allowed me the supreme pleasure of reading them all aloud.

—Jim

To C. J. Klecan and Amy Hughes, with thanks for friendship and long, late conversations.

—Cheryl

Contents at a Glance

Contents

Introduction

Welcome to the world of Narnia. We will be your tour guides. We have both read nearly everything written by C. S. Lewis, and we've read *The Chronicles of Narnia* many times. Jim even wrote a master's thesis on the man. Save your questions till the end of the tour, please. Oh, you wanted to know what we'll learn on this tour? Now that's a good question.

In the first part, we'll look at the background to the Narnian chronicles: We'll find out about the author (C. S. Lewis, a.k.a. "Jack"), get some information about fairy tales and myths, have an introduction to the land of Narnia, and even meet the great lion Aslan. (You in the back there, hiding—don't worry, Aslan is good even if he's not tame.) We'll also look at what Lewis is trying to teach us in these books.

In the second part, we'll look at *The Chronicles of Narnia* themselves, one book at a time. We'll introduce you to the most important characters of each book (yes, "most important" *is* kind of subjective), give you some hints of what you might watch for as you read the book, and even look at some books, myths and fairy tales, and Bible stories that gave Lewis some of his ideas for the book. Writing this book, we saw all sorts of things we never saw before, like how many different sources Lewis used to help him get ideas.

The Chronicles of Narnia are children's books, but don't feel bad about liking them even if you're an adult. Cheryl didn't discover these books till she was a teenager (except for that fifth-grade teacher who read *The Lion, the Witch and the Wardrobe* to the class—she thought the book was weird and the Witch a bit spooky). And now she's read the books lots of times and owns way too many copies of them.

Because they were written to children, they were written to be read aloud, so try doing that, even if you don't have a child. Jim finally got around to that with his third daughter after the first two enjoyed reading them so much. A children's author once explained that a good children's book may have sad events in it, but it must give *hope*. It can't be gloomy and sad all the way through. And these books are filled with hope and inspiration.

Why are we drawn to *The Chronicles of Narnia?* The answers might be as numerous as the readers. Many of us read everything Lewis has written. Aslan compels us. Narnia fascinates us. And we love the story. The Christian symbolism might invite, or we may read them in spite of that.

The Order to Read Them

You there, on the right, what was your question? Okay, she asked about the order in which to read the *Chronicles:*

There are two main orders. Here's the published order:

> *The Lion, the Witch and the Wardrobe*
>
> *Prince Caspian: The Return to Narnia*
>
> *The Voyage of the Dawn Treader*
>
> *The Silver Chair*
>
> *The Horse and His Boy*
>
> *The Magician's Nephew*
>
> *The Last Battle*

Then there's the order in which things happen, or the chronological order, for a total of three changes:

> *The Magician's Nephew*
>
> *The Lion, the Witch and the Wardrobe*
>
> *The Horse and His Boy*
>
> *Prince Caspian: The Return to Narnia*
>
> *The Voyage of the Dawn Treader*
>
> *The Silver Chair*
>
> *The Last Battle*

Cheryl tends to read the series in a modified version of chronological order: she reads *The Lion, the Witch and the Wardrobe,* then *Magician's*

Nephew, and then the others in chronological order. In her opinion, *Wardrobe* pretty much has to be read first, as it is the best way to get into Narnia. *The Horse and His Boy* isn't really essential to the story line (please don't tell Lewis we said that), but if you read it, it can be placed anywhere among the other books.

Extras

Throughout the book, you'll find snappy little sidebars and margin notes designed to help answer questions and illuminate the world of Narnia for you.

 God Sightings

Discusses the place of faith in Lewis's life and works.

 **Narnian Dictionary**

Defines unfamiliar words.

 Navigating Narnia

Contains background material for understanding Narnia.

 **Magic and Myth**

Offers literary links to Narnia.

Acknowledgments

To Michele Wells, our new editor at Alpha Books. Thanks for getting this book on track and for your ever-positive attitude. To Andrew Lazo, whose ideas helped set the stage for the beginning of this book. Thanks to Jim's daughter, Brigit Bell Ritchie, for gracefully adorning this book with her illustrations.

Cheryl wants to say thank you to Jim Bell, who hired her for her first after-college job, acquired her first book, assigned her some significant books to edit, and gave her the opportunity to write about Narnia, one of her favorite places.

Special Thanks to the Technical Reviewer

The Complete Idiot's Guide to the World of Narnia was reviewed by an expert who double-checked the accuracy of what you'll learn here, to help us ensure that this book gives you everything you need to know about Narnia. Special thanks are extended to Tere Stouffer.

Trademarks

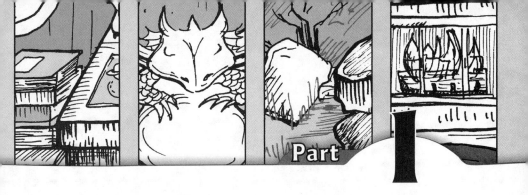

Part 1

The Land of Narnia, Its Background, and Its Author

How complicated can a series of children's books be, anyway? Well, *The Chronicles of Narnia* are easy enough that children understand them. We still think the more you know about what went into them, the better you'll understand them—and the more you'll appreciate them. So in this part, we'll look at background material: the life of C. S. Lewis (because he *wrote* them, that's why), a little bit about fairy tales and myths, and even some information about Narnia and its chief personage (lionage?), Aslan. Ready? Let's get started.

Chapter 1

A Brief Bio of C. S. Lewis: What You Need to Know and Why You Should Care

In This Chapter

- A childhood made for imagination but full of life-changing losses
- Circumstances, books, and people spurring the writing of Narnia
- A look at C. S. Lewis's life and career

How can you navigate the world of Narnia without a little info about its author? *You can't!* This chapter will provide you with just enough dates and facts to find your way around. Don't worry, we won't have a quiz at the end.

In this chapter, we give you some key biographical information about Lewis's life, including some information about how and when he wrote *The Chronicles of Narnia*. This is all with an eye to understanding what made Lewis uniquely suited to create the Narnian world.

Early Life: Jacksie, Warnie, Books, and Boxen

By all accounts, C. S. Lewis's early life was happy. Born November 29, 1898, to an attorney and a minister's daughter, his was a safe, happy world.

Call Me Jack

Clive Staples Lewis was three years younger than his only sibling, his brother, Warren ("Warnie"). The younger Lewis was called "Baby" for the first three or four years of his life. Perhaps he pondered the situation and mulled the alternatives. Would he rather be called Baby, Clive, or Staples? None of the above. (Good choice!) One day he declared he was "Jacksie." From then on, Lewis's family and friends called him "Jacksie," "Jacks," or simply "Jack."

Throughout his life, Lewis displayed a sense of self-assurance, along with an enduring talent for making his way through the world by means of words.

Brothers and Friends

Lewis shared nearly everything with Warren. The two brothers were constant companions. Throughout their lives, they remained best friends. Warren was even Lewis's first writing partner. They sometimes attended different schools, and for a few years Warren was stationed abroad in active military service. Other than that, Warren spent his whole life living in the same home as Lewis and was his closest, oldest friend.

With his brother, Lewis began writing stories as early as 1906, when he was seven. Warren created a world he called India, while Lewis busily populated Animal-Land with what he called dressed animals. These characters stood upright, smoked, and busied themselves with politics. (The stories were far more serious than *Narnia*.) Together, Lewis and Warren's world was dubbed Boxen; it occupied their imaginations for hours.

Books, Books, Books

In Lewis's autobiography, *Surprised by Joy*, or *Joy* (Harcourt Brace Jovanovich, 1955), he records that his boyhood home, Little Lea, played a key role in his development. For one thing, Lewis described his house as one in which he was guaranteed to find books that were new to him anytime he wanted—and none of them were off limits. With the frequent rainy days in Belfast, Lewis took full advantage of such an opportunity. The vast in-house library undoubtedly fueled Lewis's growing imagination.

Navigating Narnia

Lewis says that his family distrusted emotions. The family library was extensive but contained no romances or fairy tales. In some ways, Lewis had to grow up before he could become a child. And his marriage late in life really taught him the value of emotions.

Anyone Else?

Little Lea also housed Lewis's nurse, Lizzie Endicott. Lizzie contributed to the growth of Lewis's imagination by introducing him to the books of Beatrix Potter and to Irish fairy tales and stories about leprechauns. That stirred a lifetime love of such tales, a love that would later drive him to write the Narnia books.

> **Magic and Myth**
>
> Little Lea echoes throughout Narnia. In *Wardrobe*, the children's adventures begin in a rambling house loaded with books. Caspian's nurse in *Caspian* reminds us of Lizzie Endicott. *Voyage* starts in an upstairs room of the Scrubb house, where Lucy makes her way through the house to a book-lined study. Polly in *Nephew* has an attic full of tunnels much like Little Lea's.

Schoolboy Days: A Series of Losses

Settled happiness in Little Lea soon came to an end; 1908 proved a turning point.

Grandfather, Uncle—and, Most of All, Mother

In February, Lewis's mother, Flora, had a major operation for cancer. In April, Lewis's grandfather Richard Lewis died after a stroke. On August 23, his father Albert Lewis's birthday, Flora died; and the following month, Albert's brother, Lewis's Uncle Joe, died as well. But it was his mother's death that Lewis in some ways never got over.

Dead or dying mothers present some of the most poignant scenes in the *Chronicles*. In *Nephew*, Digory's mother is dying, but Aslan saves her life. In *Chair*, a green serpent kills Prince Rilian's mother. The prince's desire to avenge his mother's death leads him, unwittingly, to 10 years of slavery to his mother's killer.

Farewell to Father

Loss of a parent in youth brings a whole different dynamic to one's life. One loses the dead parent and, to some extent, the grieving parent. It was clear that Lewis felt this double loss keenly. Adults usually do better at comforting the widow than dealing with a grieving child, and Lewis must have felt very much alone in his grief.

Not only did Flora's death rob her sons of her comforting presence, but it also left the boys with Albert as their only parent. The brothers soon found their father unreliable emotionally. He certainly failed to enter into their extremely close and supportive relationship as a parent.

Sometimes he tried awkwardly to enter as one of the boys. In a sense, Flora's death caused Lewis and his brother Warren to lose *both* parents.

We're throwing around a lot of names here—why don't we take a quick roll call of key people? Each of these people—those we've met already and those we haven't—played key roles in Lewis's life and the creation of Narnia.

Seven Key People in Lewis's Life (and How They Helped Narnia)

Name	Relation to CSL	Narnian Influence
Warren Lewis	Brother	Helped Lewis create first stories as a boy
Lizzie Endicott	Nurse who told him Irish fairy and folk tales and Beatrix Potter stories	Probable model for Caspian's nurse (*Caspian*)
Albert Lewis	Father	Possible model for Erlian, father of Tirian (*Battle*)
Flora Lewis	Mother	Probable model for Digory's sick mother (*Nephew*); spurred Lewis's interest in languages
William T. Kirkpatrick	Rationalist tutor of Latin, Greek, and literary mythology	Probable model for rationalist Professor Kirke (*Wardrobe*, *Battle*)
J. R. R. Tolkien	Friend, Inklings co-founder, literary collaborator	Provided imaginative and mythic background of Narnia
Charles Williams	Friend, Inklings co-founder	Arthurian poetry; *The Place of the Lion* influenced creation of Narnia

Off to Boarding ... School?

Lewis was soon sent with his brother to a boarding school in England governed by a harsh headmaster. It was an experience of great torment for a young child who had recently lost his mother. In *Joy*, he disguises the name of the school, referring to its location as Belsen and discussing it under the subhead "Concentration Camp." The school was more about sadistic discipline than education. In fact, the headmaster was later declared insane and the school was closed. That might even top some of your own worst teachers, huh?

Rarely are schools presented positively in the *Chronicles;* even schools in Narnia are unpleasant places.

Forsaking Faith

Religion had never been all that important to Lewis as a child. He prayed and went to church, but he didn't pay much attention to that stuff. He was deeply disillusioned that his prayers for his mother had failed to influence God to save her life. Religion eventually seemed a burden that he gladly cast aside. He abandoned any interest in Christianity, although he allowed himself to be confirmed in unbelief, apparently to appease his father.

Teenage Years: Finding the Future

In the next couple years, Lewis went to two additional schools and had one term off due to illness. He hated one of these schools with a passion because of the cruelty of other boys. He also hated its compulsory games, at which he did poorly.

A Lifelong Friend

During these years, Lewis made one of the best friends of his life—and one of his most important discoveries. He went to visit a sick neighbor boy, Arthur Greeves, who was about Warren's age. To his delight, Arthur's bed table contained a copy of *Myths of the Norsemen*. The boys pored over the book together in great joy at their common interest.

Norse myths would continue to be one of Lewis's greatest loves. Many kinds of myths find their way into Narnia, as we will explore later. Throughout Lewis's life, he and Arthur corresponded regularly.

The Great Knock

Lewis had heard his father, Albert, praise the headmaster of his school, who was now tutoring. He begged to be sent to his father's old headmaster. Albert finally relented and sent Lewis to England to study with William T. Kirkpatrick. "The Great Knock" had intellectual gifts perfectly suited to Lewis. Lewis was by this time so eager to learn in isolation that he threw himself into his studies and established a pattern of reading and writing that he would follow at every opportunity for the rest of his life.

In addition to reading the Latin and Greek classics with an expert, Lewis learned how to discipline his thinking. These lessons he followed, taught, and incorporated into all of his subsequent writing. Perhaps we can glimpse an example of this training in *Wardrobe* in the interview of Susan and Peter with the Professor, who exclaims gruffly about the importance of logical thought.

Kirkpatrick found Lewis's literary taste and ability with classical languages almost unprecedented. Lewis found in Kirkpatrick's rigorously rational teaching just the sort of discipline he wanted most. He was trained in not just making conversation, but also meaning something by what he said. We can trace to this period Lewis's tendency to say only what he meant, to say it clearly, and then to move on. Such a style made Lewis the kind of storyteller who could capture and sustain attention over several books.

Books and More Books

Lewis continued developing his imaginative tastes. A scholarly boy with spending money, he grew his personal library in this time period. Lewis filled his letters to his friend Arthur Greeves with descriptions of books—he loved the covers of well-bound books almost as much as their contents. Lewis's imaginative reading at this time set the stage for much of his work to follow.

That was a good thing. In a letter to Lewis's father, Kirkpatrick confided that Lewis was fit to be only a writer or a scholar.

Morris and MacDonald

Two authors stand out from Lewis's extensive reading during his teen years: William Morris and George MacDonald. Both wrote *fantasies* and *romances*, two genres that Lewis enjoyed reading and that had not yet fallen out of literary favor.

> **Narnian Dictionary**
>
> Stories employing supernatural elements as a central part of their plot are called **fantasies.** Such stories go back thousands of years. Morris and MacDonald are key modern authors, as are Lewis and Tolkien.
>
> **Romances** were originally medieval stories about knights and classical heroes, often with supernatural elements. Many revisions of such tales were written in the nineteenth century.

In Morris (1834–1896), Lewis found a kindred spirit. Morris, who was an artist and a craftsman, wrote a number of novels and long poems that featured topics Lewis loved, including Greek heroes, Norse myth, and Arthurian romance.

MacDonald had a profound effect on Lewis. After picking up a copy of *Phantastes*, Lewis soon found the novel baptizing his imagination. It opened him up to holiness as a literary quality in a way he wouldn't fully understand until his conversion. In a sense, MacDonald laid the foundation for Lewis's beliefs and writings. At one point, Lewis claims never to have written a book in which he didn't refer to MacDonald.

> **God Sighting**
>
> George MacDonald (1824–1905) was a Scottish novelist and writer of fairy stories for adults and children. *Phantastes: A Faerie Romance* (1858) was Lewis's introduction to his writing. At Lewis's first reading, he rejected MacDonald's faith, yet he found his fairyland compelling, infused with something he later recognized as goodness. Narnia is much less topsy-turvy than MacDonald's fairyland, but the goodness of Lewis's own vision compels us.

Up to Oxford

For the rest of his life, Lewis attempted to keep his daily routine of studying, reading, and writing. But his tranquility at Kirkpatrick's was soon interrupted. First, Lewis excelled in his studies to such a degree that he won a scholarship to Oxford. Second, Lewis decided to join the ranks of the British Army as World War I continued. A native of Ireland, he was under no obligation to do so, but Warren had settled on a career as a military officer and Lewis soon followed him into the service.

Once There Was a War

By the middle of 1917, Lewis had joined the army. After Officers' Training Corps, he received a commission as a second lieutenant in the Somerset Light Infantry.

Good Company

Lewis arrived at the front lines in France on his nineteenth birthday. His war service threw him in with men of all classes, a new thing for the upper-middle-class young man. In the army, Lewis commanded and worked with men from every walk of life. Perhaps we can attribute the difference in tone between Mr. Tumnus's urbanity and the Beavers' down-home earthiness to the social mixing that took place in the trenches.

Mercifully, the war ended soon for Lewis, due to shrapnel from a misguided English explosive. After stints in the hospital for trench fever and the shrapnel injury, his service was over.

Lewis's war service, although relatively short and safe, marked him for the rest of his life. Nightmares plagued him, and nearly every one of his stories contained conflict and battle. Each of the Narnian chronicles contains at least one battle, although in *Nephew*, the battle is background; Charn has been decimated by war before we arrive. Lewis compared trench warfare to the Battle of Troy as described in *The Iliad*.

Literary Life in the Trenches

Even in war, Lewis was able to maintain a literary life. Lewis's correspondence with his father and others speaks more about the books he managed to read and the men with whom he discussed them than the horrors of war.

Not long after his war service, Lewis had a collection of poems accepted for publication, and his father helped him create the title: *Spirits in Bondage* (William Henemann, 1919). This achieved little notice (and apparently little or no financial reward) for Lewis. Although disappointed, Lewis nevertheless continued to write poetry, hoping to find his place in the literary world. How little could he have guessed that great fame awaited him as a writer of fairy tales rather than of poems. When the war ended safely for both the Lewis brothers, Lewis returned to Oxford to begin a brilliant scholarly career.

Navigating Narnia

On two occasions, Lewis chose to use a pseudonym. For his first book of poetry, *Spirits in Bondage*, he published using the name Clive Hamilton. *A Grief Observed*, written after his wife died, was published with the pseudonym N. W. Clerk until after his own death.

Back to Oxford

Brilliant though he was in literary undertakings, Lewis could hardly add a column of numbers. He failed to pass the math portion of Responsions, an entrance exam required of Oxford students. Fortunately for Lewis (and all his future readers), Responsions was waived for veterans, and Lewis took his place at Oxford after completing his military service.

Excellent Education

The university system at Oxford and Cambridge has two levels of instructors: professors and dons (also known as tutors or fellows). All instructors must give a series of lectures and must publish scholarly works. But while professors get to stop there, dons have a whole lot of work left to do. They have to tutor a number of undergraduates every week.

Unlike the classroom experience American undergrads experience, undergrads at Oxford and Cambridge meet with a tutor once a week, reading aloud the 10-page essay they've written during the week. The tutors then advise their students on how to improve their thinking and writing, recommending books and lecture series. The students follow the don's advice during the week, write another essay, and repeat the process every week in the term.

This goes on for three years, after which students take long examinations on the subjects covered. In the end, they receive a ranked degree, First through Fourth Class in Lewis's day. One might compare a First Class degree from Oxford to graduating summa cum laude with a Bachelor's degree from Harvard. That's the tutorial process Lewis faced at Oxford. Doesn't that help you understand the relationship between Dr. Cornelius and Prince Caspian (portrayed in *Caspian*) a little better?

Third Time's the Charm

During Lewis's education at Oxford, he took *three* degrees with First Class honors, first in Greek and Latin literature and next in ancient philosophy and history. To top it off, Lewis completed the entire three-year program in English in one year. By anyone's standards, a "triple-First" was a remarkable achievement.

In the intellectual community at Oxford, Lewis found his true element. He won essay prizes, was elected to elite literary societies, and enjoyed great academic success. All of these factors seemed to point to a rich and successful academic career as a don and later a professor.

And indeed he found such success, but it came slowly. Two years after his First in English, he was elected to be a fellow of Magdalen College at Oxford. In that role, he tutored English for the next 29 years. Scholars in English still see many of Lewis's academic articles and books as landmarks in their fields of study.

A New Friend

After taking his third degree and finding a position that allowed him to specialize in medieval and Renaissance English literature, Lewis began to widen his group of friends. One new friend, J. R. R. Tolkien

(1892–1973), remained a solid friend for the rest of his days. Tolkien had a profound effect on the course of Lewis's life, and Lewis in turn became a key figure in helping Tolkien create *The Lord of the Rings* (LOTR). Their friendship, however, did not start out very positively.

The day he met Tolkien, the professor of Anglo-Saxon language, Lewis recorded his impressions in his diary, noting that a good smack would set him right. But Tolkien shared Lewis's lifelong love of Norse mythology. So when Tolkien started the Coalbiters, a study group in Old Norse that read all the old myths in their original tongue, Lewis gladly joined. Thus began one of the most important literary friendships of the twentieth century.

True Myth: Finding Faith

Lewis and Tolkien soon discovered that they loved *mythology* in very different ways, which related closely to their approach to Christianity. Lewis was still an atheist, although he was beginning to have some doubts about his beliefs. He loved myths, but he understood them to be lies, however beautiful and stirring. Tolkien saw Lewis's view as pure nonsense. A deeply committed Roman Catholic, Tolkien saw mythology as stories splintered from one true myth, found in the story of Jesus. One night their differences came to a head in a way that changed Lewis's whole world (and perhaps many worlds after him).

Narnian Dictionary

Mythology is an extremely old genre centering on gods, heroes, and creation, and is often used to explain natural events and to help form society. Based on a specific cultural heritage, usually handed down orally, myth can have a haunting effect on readers. Homer and Hesiod (in Greek) and Ovid and Virgil (in Latin) are perhaps its most famous authors.

Tolkien pointed out to Lewis that Lewis loved myth anywhere he saw it, especially the myth of a god who dies and rises again. Whether Osiris (from Egyptian myth) or Odin and Balder (Norse myth), anytime Lewis met the theme of the dying and rising god, he found himself strangely, deeply moved. And what, Tolkien asked, was Christianity except that very same myth that had actually occurred in a certain place and at a certain time in history?

A few nights later, Lewis reluctantly knelt and admitted his belief in God. Two years later, he further converted from *theism* to Christianity. There, finally, his lifelong spiritual struggle came to an end ... and to a beginning. Only after becoming a Christian and abandoning the pride of literary ambition did Lewis's writing career really begin.

> **Narnian Dictionary**
>
> **Theism** is a belief in a god. Not all religions are theistic; Buddhism doesn't believe in the existence of any god. And being a theist doesn't necessarily mean believing in a god who is currently involved in human affairs.

Lewis admits in his autobiography that for some time before his conversion, he struggled with the awareness that the majority of his very favorite authors were Christians. He'd find a new favorite author, only to find this disturbing trait in him as well. He reports that it began to feel as though all his books were turning against him. Eventually he surrendered, but only because he felt he couldn't decently do anything else.

It might be interesting to note that the Bible contains stories of two men whose lives were similar to Lewis's in several regards: Moses in the Old Testament, and the apostle Paul in the New Testament. Like Lewis, both received the very best education of their days. Both resisted God when He showed up in their lives. (Paul was blind for three days after his encounter with Jesus!) And both wrote extensively after their conversion: Moses wrote the first five books of the Old Testament, and Paul wrote almost a third of the New Testament.

Making Many Myths: The Inklings

Along with fellow Coalbiter Nevill Coghill, Lewis and Tolkien formed a group that came to replace their gathering of devotees to Norse myth. The Inklings began to meet to give members an audience for their own original writings, usually works in progress. In the Inklings, both men seemed to find their stride as writers.

Tolkien began to read aloud from his extensive mythology, part of which he would publish as *The Hobbit* and *The Lord of the Rings*. Lewis loved Tolkien's mythology. Tolkien later credited Lewis's pressure and encouragement with forcing him to make a narrative out of his materials. After many years of stops and restarts and numerous drafts, Tolkien published *The Hobbit* (in 1937). *The Lord of the Rings* followed much later (1952–1954).

We don't mean to imply that the Inklings meetings were dry, scholarly gatherings—quite the opposite. Men met as friends, with much laughter and good cheer. They soon decided that one meeting a week wasn't enough. Many of their meetings were held in a pub, the Eagle and Child, unofficially called the Bird and Baby. Think of men listening to other men reading stories and being able to comment and rib each other, with a little drinking and a few pipes in the mix. That's not quite so dull, is it?

Friends and Publishing

After the 1936–1937 appearances of Lewis's scholarly *Allegory of Love* and Tolkien's *The Hobbit*, both men turned to the writing that would occupy most of their time in the 1940s. While Tolkien labored away at "The New Hobbit" (LOTR), Lewis published several books, including his Space Trilogy (or Interplanetary Romances): *Out of the Silent Planet* (1938), *Perelandra* (1943), and *That Hideous Strength* (1945). This successful publication of otherworldly fiction undoubtedly set the stage for his children's fairy tales about Narnia in the next decade.

Magic and Myth

In Lewis's *Out of the Silent Planet*, a man, Ransom, is abducted and sent to Malacandra (or Mars). Ransom finds three different forms of intelligent life.

Perelandra finds Ransom traveling to the planet known to us as Venus. Its almost-human first woman is about to be bombarded by temptation.

That Hideous Strength is the longest and most philosophical book. It deals with scientific issues akin to genetic engineering.

After the bombing of London, children from the city began to be sent to outlying cities for protection. The Lewis brothers' home (called "the Kilns") hosted several groups of children. Lewis's personal experience with the evacuated children probably provided him the imaginative setting of the beginning of *Wardrobe*, in which the four Pevensie children flee London and make their way to the old house of Professor Kirke.

Writing It Up

Lewis was having many dreams of lions. Perhaps this was partly from the recent death of Inklings member Charles Williams, whose *Place of the Lion* (1933) had sparked friendship between the two men. Lewis appears to have written a draft of the opening paragraph of *Wardrobe* several years earlier. Late in 1948, not long after completing a volume of *Essays Presented to Charles Williams*, Lewis took up the story again.

During his teenage years, Lewis had a picture pop into his head of a faun walking through a snowy wood carrying packages and an umbrella. When he was around 50, he began to try to write it up. The image of the faun, along with a picture of a white queen on a sleigh, began to come together in the form of a fairy tale. Once he began writing, the golden lion Aslan came rushing in, giving Lewis purpose and meaning for the story. By 1953, all seven of the Narnian tales were complete (although not all had yet been published). Lewis had planned to write just one, but image led to image and book led to book. Lewis was delighted to be writing just the sort of tales he most enjoyed reading.

Lewis wrote the books at the end of very long days. He continued giving lectures and tutoring students, and he helped run the household at the Kilns. He also wrote *Surprised by Joy* and his 800-plus-page volume on the sixteenth century for the *Oxford History of English Literature*. After publishing *The Screwtape Letters*, a book of "letters" from a senior demon to a junior tempter about the best ways to tempt a human, Lewis had become a spokesman for Christianity and was in great demand. His BBC radio broadcasts during World War II made Lewis the best-known voice on the radio after Winston Churchill, and he then compiled the series of BBC lectures into *Mere Christianity*.

The seven *Chronicles* are probably his most enduring imaginative legacy. They have never gone out of print and have sold millions of copies. Indeed, with the advent of the twenty-first-century movie versions of the *Chronicles*, Lewis's popularity continues to swell with readers of all stripes, children and adults alike.

By the end of the 1940s, books had begun to explode out of Lewis's pen. (And by the way, Lewis continued to the end of his days to write by dipping a pen in ink.) Lewis put out 13 books in the 1950s, more than 40 essays, more than 90 poems, and 12 book reviews. Keep in mind how busy he was. Lewis had to lecture and publish while also tutoring students. In addition, hundreds of people were now writing to him. He faithfully answered each letter, eventually with Warren's help.

You certainly can't accuse Lewis of being a slacker. We must see *The Chronicles of Narnia* as Lewis's release from long days of labor. And for millions of children and adults, they have provided an entry point into an enchanted otherworld.

After Narnia: Success at Last

Academic excellence and hard work weren't enough to bring Lewis success at Oxford. He never did become a full professor there, and most scholars believe it was because of his Christian faith, which fellow academics found to be an unscholarly embarrassment. But by 1954, almost everything had changed for Lewis.

A Professor at Last

A position as professor (in medieval and Renaissance literature) was created for him at Cambridge. That gave him both more money and more time to write. After 29 years, he was freed from the heavy load of tutoring. And none too soon, for his responsibilities were increasing, and soon his health began to fail.

Increasing Correspondence

With greater fame came a special burden—daily correspondence from all over the world. Each letter received a personal response. Some turned into ongoing correspondence, including one with an American lady and fellow author, Joy Davidman, who would become important to Lewis.

The publication of *The Chronicles of Narnia*, children's books written by a confirmed bachelor with no nieces and nephews and little contact with children, brought Lewis eager letters from curious children. He answered each with respect, never talking down to them.

Magic and Myth

For more insight into Lewis and the *Chronicles*, check out the superb *Letters to Children* (Macmillan, 1985). Many times he gave his young readers writing advice on the stories they sent for his evaluation, praising their description or pointing out flaws in word choice and logic. He also answered their questions about Narnia, Aslan, and the Pevensie children.

Less Public Speaking

The audiences for his books were greater than the numbers he could reach by speaking, Lewis believed, so he cut back on his public speaking to focus more on his writing. Many of his lectures were published in books; quite a few of those books were published after his death.

The Reach of the *Chronicles*

The extreme popularity of the *Chronicles* came slowly. Lewis originally intended to write only *Wardrobe*, but demand moved him to turn his masterpiece into a series. Yet many parents and educators felt the book was really too scary for children. Today their popularity with adults and children continues to grow, and they are available in many forms, from simplified storybooks to audio and video versions. Translated into more than 30 languages, with more than 85 million copies in print, they are among the best-selling children's books of all time.

A Grief Observed: From Bachelor to Widower

In his fifties, Lewis met Joy Davidman, whom he later married—twice. Joy was a writer herself and a fan with whom he had corresponded.

Lewis's books had a lot to do with her conversion to Christianity. Her journey from a Jewish background to atheism and activism in the Communist party, and then to embracing Christianity might remind you of Lewis's own journey to faith.

A Marriage of Convenience

Joy was an American who decided she wanted to live in England. She and Lewis had become good friends during her stay. Her visa was expiring. Lewis, who believed in a distinction between a legal, civic marriage and a church marriage, did her a large favor by marrying her and thus extending his British citizenship to her. Then he went on with his bachelor life. Perhaps they would never have had a "real" marriage if she had stayed healthy. But cancer soon struck Joy.

Joy's connection to Narnia is relatively slim. Before he married Joy, Lewis had dedicated *The Horse and His Boy* to Joy's sons from her first marriage, David and Douglas Gresham. Douglas went on to write an autobiography of life with Lewis and his mother, and has played a central role in transforming the *Chronicles* into movies. But Doug, his brother, and Joy arrived in person in Lewis's life after he had finished writing the world of Narnia, although it certainly was a real place in their imaginations.

A Marriage of Love—and Loss

With Joy in the hospital with cancer, Lewis began to realize his love for his legal bride. He found a preacher to marry them in a Christian ceremony at her hospital bed—expecting her to live only a few more days or weeks. God gave her four additional years. Lewis took her home, and they even had a honeymoon and a trip to Greece.

Magic and Myth

If you want to know more about Lewis's life, biographies abound. He himself wrote three books that are autobiographical. *Surprised by Joy* is his life story. *Pilgrim's Regress* (1933) is a novel, an allegory like *Pilgrim's Progress*, but it's widely believed to be Lewis's own conversion told in story form. And *A Grief Observed* (1961) tells of his sorrow at the loss of his wife.

Joy helped inspire his novel *Till We Have Faces* (1956); became one of Lewis's closest friends; and then, when they fell in love and married, made some of his last years the happiest time of his life. Sadly, the happiness of Lewis's life with Joy ended all too soon. The cancer came back and he lost her in 1960—one of the deepest griefs of his life. His own health went downhill fast after her death. The screenplay and movie *Shadowlands* is a revised telling of their brief life together.

Lewis's Death

Lewis continued lecturing until health problems led him to resign his Cambridge professorship. In 1963, health problems plagued him for most of the year. Finally, on November 22, 1963 (within hours of the assassination of John F. Kennedy), Lewis died in bed, one week shy of his sixty-fifth birthday. Warren, who lived most of his life with his brother, discovered him in his bed. He never got over his grief of losing his brother and best friend.

Posthumous Publishing

In the years since Lewis's death, many books of his essays, poetry, and letters have been released. The content of some overlaps, so it is impossible to give a precise figure of the number of books written by C. S. Lewis. But his output was immense, and he wrote successfully in multiple genres. In addition, hundreds of books and academic papers have been written *about* him and his work. See the appendix for a small sample of some good ones.

A Continuing Legacy

Lewis's books continue to draw new readers every year, young and old alike. As movies pull fans into theaters and new editions of his books pour off the presses, this trend is expected to continue for some years to come. And for many, their first, youthful introduction to Lewis remains their favorite—the tales of a magical land called Narnia.

Key Dates and Periods in Lewis's Life

Date	Significance	So What?
November 29, 1898	Lewis born	Umm … do you have to ask?
1908	Lewis's mother, paternal grandfather, and uncle all die	Lewis turns from faith and from his father; turns to Warren
1914–1918	Private tutoring; World War I service; begins studies at Oxford	Key period of intellectual and social growth
1925–1926	Gets job teaching English at Oxford; meets, befriends J. R. R. Tolkien	Stays at this job for 29 years; Tolkien influences Lewis in several ways
1931–1933	Becomes theist, then Christian	Books begin to flow from his pen
1942	*The Screwtape Letters* published	One of his best-known works, the book that made his name known
1950–1956	*The Chronicles of Narnia* published	Finds comfort: love, financial security, professorship at Cambridge
April 23, 1956	Marries Joy Davidman (who dies July 13, 1960)	Bachelor Lewis had long since published his autobiography, *Surprised by Joy*
November 22, 1963	Lewis dies peacefully	Same day as Aldous Huxley (*Brave New World*) and John F. Kennedy died

The Least You Need to Know

- Lewis was an atheist for his early adult years, although many of his favorite books were written by Christians.

- Many of Lewis's friends were fellow authors, including J. R. R. Tolkien, who helped Lewis convert from atheism to Christianity in his thirties.

- Lewis's lifelong interest in myth and his friendships set the stage for the writing of *The Chronicles of Narnia*.

Chapter 2

Myths and Fairy Tales, and Their Place in Narnia

In This Chapter

- The significance of myth in history and in Narnia
- An introduction to the fairy tale, and some reasons Lewis used this genre to write about Narnia
- A few thoughts on medieval times and their relevance to our day

Human societies have always understood themselves through story: true history, myth, and tales of all sorts. Oral cultures use myth more than literate cultures do, but mythology has affected the way all of us see the world.

Myths and fairy tales are more than ways to entertain children. They express a culture's values, help people understand how actions meet their natural consequences, and help people make sense of the world.

Lewis came to believe that myth can even express truth. That is, myth as a fictionalized way of looking at the world is a mirror of "true myth": the story of Jesus Christ, which is almost too large to be taken in all at once. We can come to understand bits and pieces of the true story as we get to know myth and fairy tales. Lewis's *The Chronicles of Narnia* were infused with hints of this true myth and with pieces of myths and fairy tales from many cultures.

Defining Myth

Mythology is a story form that makes sense of big questions, such as birth and death, creation, and suffering. Cultures use myth to figure out and define humanity's relation to the supernatural, other people, and the natural world. Myth was first put in written form by the Sumerians, about 2500 B.C.E. The three major forms of myth in the West are Greek, Roman, and Norse. Hindu myth is another important form, and many other cultures have myths. Myth is largely oral, handed down through generations and heavily based on stories of mankind's interactions with the gods. As we'll see throughout this book, Narnia owes much of its character to myth, particularly Greek and Norse myth and Arthurian myth and legend.

Not Necessarily a Lie

We tend to use the word *myth* to mean something that isn't true. (In *Wardrobe*, that was the meaning in the title of a book in Tumnus's library *Is Man a Myth?*) But as a literary category, sometimes it is hard to figure out where myth overlaps with a culture's true history. What tales of King Arthur are really true? Is the story of the Trojan horse based on an actual event? Did Washington chop down that cherry tree? But deeper than questions of whether specific events are true and how heavily they have been embroidered, myths shape people's cultural identity and the way they look at the world.

Ancient people told myth as their history, making little distinction between what really happened and what was fictionalized. The myths looked at universal truths common to humanity: longings and fears, birth and death, creation and destruction, the battle against evil.

All cultures that have myths have creation myths. The story of a great flood that nearly destroys mankind is told in many myths, hinting of the flood told as history in the book of Genesis. Myths helped people understand mysteries, giving personalities to the stars and putting the history of one's own people into a bigger picture. One's tribal gods became part of the same myths with gods believed to rule other lands.

Gods and Heroes of Myth and Legend

Myth was not religiously significant in the sense of being an aid to worship. The gods of mythology are not, as a rule, man's masters, and they are not the means to his salvation. They are superior to him and worthy of fear and attempts at appeasement, but they do not seek a relationship with him. (Compare this sense of distance with the Christian God or with Aslan.) Many of the myths show dualism—good gods battling bad gods, or gods that have good and evil roles, such as the Hindu god Shiva. Besides their place as sacred history, myths show people their social history.

Edith Hamilton's classic *Mythology* (Little, Brown and Company, 1942) gives useful background to mythology and also retells many myths. Hamilton says myth was not created by primitive people who saw a strange, beautiful world in the forest, but by civilized poets who felt terror there. Mythology shows a world of capricious gods appeased by great sacrifice, including human sacrifice.

Myths were told and retold, often by poets or professional traveling storytellers. (Lewis uses such a storyteller in *Chair*, who tells the story of "the horse and his boy," soon to be told in book form by Lewis.) The Greeks had large open-air theaters that were used in this way.

Myth also functioned as *allegory*, with recognizable, symbolic characters giving easy "hints" to a story's meaning. Such *archetypes* show up in much of the world's literature, even today. Lions still represent courage and leadership (which makes exceptions such as the Cowardly Lion in *The Wizard of Oz* all the more compelling), and coyotes and foxes represent deceit and treachery.

Narnian Dictionary

Allegory is an extended metaphor, usually book length, characterized by a one-to-one correspondence of every element. One character may represent suffering, and another may represent joy, for instance. Allegory is often associated with biblical interpretation, most famously in John Bunyan's *Pilgrim's Progress* (1678). The *Chronicles* are definitively *not* allegories.

An **archetype** is an element used by multiple storytellers with the same meaning. A dragon, for instance, not only flies, breathes fire, and fights violently, but also hoards gold—thus it is used as an archetypal symbol of greed. Archetypes help people understand and remember stories, which is especially true in a culture where stories are passed on orally rather than through books.

Related Story Forms

Many other types of stories are related to myth:

- **Folk tales**—Have mythic elements, but on a smaller scale than myths. (Remember Paul Bunyan and his great blue ox, Babe?) Generally, they deal with conflicts between people and reveal a moral truth.

- **Legends**—Present "bigger than life" pictures of some historical character or event, but are not incorporated into a culture's belief system as myth is.

- **Fables**—Have a clear-cut moral that is stated directly, as part of an obviously fictional tale (think of those by Aesop).

- **Epics**—(One of Lewis's favorite genres.) Long, serious poems telling the story of heroes. *The Iliad* and *The Odyssey* and Milton's *Paradise Lost* are epics. (Ballads are usually shorter than epics and are made to be sung and accompanied by dance, just in case you were wondering.)

What Lewis Liked About Myth

From the time he was a boy, Lewis was drawn to the mystery of myth. He never abandoned his love for it; one of the last books he wrote was a novel-length retelling of a myth. The power of myth compelled him for many reasons.

Numinous

Lewis and Tolkien were both very much drawn to the numinous. The word numinous refers to the sense of a presence different, powerful, and terribly good. (When the Pevensie children first met Aslan in *Wardrobe*, they realized it's possible for a being to be both terrible and good.)

Although Lewis was deeply moved by the numinous in George MacDonald and in other writers, it didn't fully make sense to him until his conversion. If you want a quick example of it, flip over to Chapter 7 of *Wardrobe*, where the children first hear the name Aslan. You also get a sense of it in Chapter 10 when they meet the real Father Christmas. Their response is very somber and, at the same time, deeply joyful. If you know *The Lord of the Rings*, you'll find a similar quality in the encounter with Galadriel in Lothlorien.

Lewis said he believed in Christianity as he believed in the sun—not only because he saw it, but because by it he saw everything else. Before his conversion, he loved myth, but after his conversion, he understood it. He saw the bigger stories behind it.

Striking Deeply

Myth is a story form that looks at really significant issues of life and death, interactions with the supernatural, and good and evil. It attempts to answer important "why" questions. Lewis cut to the heart of a matter rather than being distracted by the trivial. A man's man and a serious thinker, he respected and was moved by stories that had survived centuries or millennia of looking at hard questions. Once he realized the connection between myth's stories of creation and the biblical account—the stories of the dying and rising god and the one who had really died and come alive—and knew that God really had communicated with man, he was free to "believe" myth and not just enjoy it. He could see where it really pointed.

 God Sighting

Lewis's concept of yearning or longing, which he called Joy, was powerful in his life. Also called *sehnsucht* (German), the search for greater experiences of the longing ended in his becoming a Christian. Lewis came to realize that our deepest longings are for God, and even for the Christian, they are not fully met in this life.

Lewis argued that the pagan who believes in myths is closer to truth than the modern person who disbelieves everything. He was comfortable as a Christian using pagan myth, believing that it was at least making humans stop and consider their relation with the supernatural. Because myth had played a major role in his conversion, he knew that God could use stories of man-invented gods in others' lives as well. Myth presents a world larger than our everyday concerns.

Inevitability

As we read biographies or look back at the full history of a person's life, we can often see a pattern developing. Only in retrospect do children's early interests make their eventual career choice obvious. Only as we see a full biography of a person, or a full history of a culture, do we see how all the pieces fit together into a whole.

Myth is large enough to show us the big picture, the inevitable results of certain actions. Lewis appreciated that sense that actions matter and that choices have clear consequences, for life is not haphazard. Behind all of life is an Author who knows how all our choices will come together for better or for worse. In fact, Romans 8:28 in the New Testament guarantees that all things in Christians' lives work together for good, even if they don't look good at the time.

Magic and Myth

Lewis's *Till We Have Faces* is unlike any of his other fiction—it's based on the myth of Psyche and Cupid. The book was suggested by Joy Davidman, who became his wife the year he published it.

A Few Notes on Mythologies

Much of Western culture is rooted in myths. As we'll see when we look briefly at the Middle Ages, the days of the week and the planets are named for the pagan deities who come to life through myth. Myths affect our lives in numerous ways, from our language and literature to the way we look at the world.

"An Apple-Laden Land": Greek and Roman Myth

Greek gods were made in the image of their inventors. They married and had families. They had human vices and virtues. Greeks thought humans were the highest point of creation, the most beautiful beings. Though their gods were fearsome, they also could be treated fairly casually, with familiarity, and even laughed at. Zeus had many affairs, making his wife Hera jealous. The mighty winged horse Pegasus was stabled at night in Corinth like any ordinary horse. Greek mythology was more a form of science and literature than religion, a method of exploring the meaning of the world, according to Edith Hamilton.

Each city-state in Greece had its own local gods, and with them its own religious festivals and myths. The most important gods were incorporated into the mythology of all of Greece. Greek gods were modified into Roman gods, with new Roman names: for example, Zeus became Jupiter; Ares became Mars; Aphrodite became Venus (see any gods through your telescope lately?). Also, Artemis became Diana; Dionysus became Bacchus; and Eros became Cupid.

Of Courtly Mice and Men: Arthurian Myth

In Britain, schoolchildren learned myths that came much closer to home: the myths or legends of King Arthur, his knights of the round table, and the quest for the Holy Grail. (*Voyage* presents its own quest, as does *Chair*.) Stories of Merlin enchanted schoolchildren and made their way into fiction.

Lewis had double reason to use Arthurian imagery in his tales: growing up in Ireland and spending his adult life in England, the tales would have been very familiar, and they resonated with his medieval scholarship. Thus we see the mouse Reepicheep, a miniature medieval knight, in *Caspian* and *Voyage*. For Reepicheep, honor comes above anything else; he is motivated by his courage and his desire to reach his own personal quest—the utter east and Aslan's country.

Wolves and White Witches: Norse Myth

Norse myth referred to the mythology of the Scandinavian people, a thoroughly developed mythology that included stories all the way from creation to the destruction of the gods. Lewis loved Norse myth, and his friend J. R. R. Tolkien based much of *The Lord of the Rings* on it. Beings in the myths included gods and goddesses, fates, elves, giants, dwarfs, humans, and beasts—and white witches, like the one who ended up in Narnia.

An important feature of Norse mythology is the world ash tree, Yggdrasil. It has three roots, and the disk (not sphere) of the world rests in its branches. Its gods included Odin and his wife, Frigg; Thor; Balder; and the trickster Loki. (Tuesday through Friday on our calendar come from the Viking gods Tyr, Odin, Thor, and Frigg.) The mythology was put into written form by Christian historians, so its earlier forms are uncertain. The mythology is grave and solemn, which would have appealed to Lewis.

Myth Made Fact: Christianity

Myth remains myth even when it is a fact, just as we can say that a couple has a "fairy-tale wedding" without meaning that their wedding didn't really happen. Lewis found that Christianity has similar themes to the greatest of the myths, with the added beauty of its being true.

Authors have sometimes found that evil is easier to present in a life-like, interesting way than good is. We equate niceness and gentleness with goodness, and niceness and gentleness can seem weak in a story. Even strength can be misrepresented as weakness when stories get retold. Think Jesus was sort of a wimp? Then you haven't read the New Testament lately. The real Jesus knocked over tables in the temple, called leaders by harsh names like "hypocrite" or "whitewashed tomb," and willingly went to a death so frightening that His sweat became bloody as He even thought about it.

The Jewish people, who gave us the Bible, were a thoroughly monotheistic people (believing in one God). They were very careful not to make images depicting God. The Jewish Scriptures (the Old Testament) were very carefully recorded as history, without the exaggeration and literary effect associated with myth. Interestingly, the Jews themselves did not have a mythology of a dying god, and the idea is a difficult one for Jews to accept, even today. Though Jesus was Jewish, most Jews reject Him as the Jewish Messiah He claimed to be.

A Dying God Comes to Life

Christianity is a belief that takes evil very seriously, to the point that human evil resulted in the death of God. In it, the strong do not win; the winners are those who submit themselves to God, who Himself submitted to death for our sakes. The ultimate happy ending comes because the dying God returned to life.

In Lewis's essay "Myth Became Fact" in *God in the Dock* (Eerdmans, 1970), he says that Christianity is both perfect myth and perfect fact. God claims not only our love and obedience, but also our wonder and delight. Without feeding on the Bible as a delight, we quickly limit Christianity to a series of facts, like a dry history text. Aslan reminds us that good is something compelling, something we want to be near and to imitate.

A true story can be large enough to be mythical—that is, a story that encompasses other stories, symbolizing great truths and explaining the world. The Bible is more than myth, but it is not less. Thus, Narnia encompasses Bible truths as well as those of the great myths.

So What Are Fairy Tales, Anyway?

The majority of fairy tales available in the West come from three collections: those written down by Charles Perrault, the Brothers Grimm, and Hans Christian Andersen. In modern understanding, fairy tales are children's stories—written to delight and entertain. But they were also written to instruct, and they weren't always thought of as a genre for children. Fairy tales show a world that is unlike our own in one very important point, and not the most obvious one: in the best fairy tales, good is always rewarded and evil always meets its just due.

In *Letters to Children*, Lewis says "a great romance is like a flower whose smell reminds you of something you can't quite place." Adults are more likely to have that sense than children do, so the child to whom Lewis wrote might not have understood him. But fairy tales remind one of life itself. They fit life's keyhole.

The Connection Between Myth and Fairy Tales

The Brothers Grimm believed that folk tales, or fairy tales, were the vestiges of ancient myths, but without the religious significance. The supernatural folk in fairy tales are not gods; the primary characters are people and "long livers," or mythical beings.

The Land of Faery

The use of the word *fairy* in fairy tales can be confusing. Few fairy tales include the beings known as fairies. (Narnia doesn't.) *Faery* is actually a *place* that has been described as an alternate Britain. It's life seen through a mirror, populated by nonhuman beings. Faery has been called the "Perilous Realm," and in most of its stories, it is not a good place for human beings. In the tales with fairies and elves, ordinary humans find their bedrooms turned into flowery pastures, complete with trees and streams. Without going anywhere, they have ended up in faery.

Whether fairies, dwarfs, giants, or talking beasts, the nonhuman creatures in faery don't usually seek out human beings unless they have need of them. (Fairies themselves desire a mortal as king in many stories.) Humans want to hold communion with other races, and they may seek faery, but it is not home to human beings. It's wisest not to linger in its forests after dark. As Mr. Beaver reminded the Pevensie children, some of the trees are on the wrong side.

Navigating Narnia

Which is correct, *dwarfs* or *dwarves*? *Dwarf* had always been made plural as *dwarfs*, but language expert Tolkien didn't think that matched the way English made other plurals. He decided to use the plural *dwarves* in his books. Disney apparently agreed (*Snow White and the Seven Dwarves*). Most literature from before the 1960s, including the *Chronicles*, uses *dwarfs*.

The Meaning of Fairy Tales

Like myths, fairy tales tend to follow set themes and grand narratives. They, too, have archetypes, often overlapping with those of myths. Only a few fairy tales are well known in the West today, and many of them deal with male and female behavior. Marriage is the prize for virtue (for women) or a successful quest (usually for men). In fairy tales, good always conquers evil, and good and evil are easily differentiated. The forces of evil often hold the upper hand for most of the story, with incredible handicaps or burdens facing the hero or heroine.

Fairy tales are infused with magic, often of the harmful kind. They have many common elements, including frequent use of stepmothers, enchanted animals, cannibal witches, archetypal creatures, and prohibitions and binding promises. Though often brutal and violent, their horror takes place in a different world. Many experts have argued that children who live in our violent world can face their fears better through seeing them in exaggerated form in fairy land, where good wins out over evil, and where the story has an otherworldly feel that lends some distance from the fear. No one *really* wants to meet Jadis, Narnia's White Witch.

Fairy tales present a world that is sometimes confusing and topsy-turvy from our perspective: cows wait years to be milked, witches hire housemaids to eat, and gold and jewels lay in sacks. But the fairy-tale world has purpose and order. Fairy tales offer social and moral guidelines, and express the values by which we wish to live—which may explain why many of today's fairy tales are, in fact, mockeries of the boy-seeks-girl, virtue-triumphs-over-evil model. That is no longer what our culture desires.

Hero(ines): Good and Bad

Fairy tales often present moral choices to the hero and help the reader learn to make good choices. Through fairy tales, readers can see the basic human issues, simplified and boiled down. In our day, fairy tales are usually published as stories for children. That hasn't always been the case, and Lewis and Tolkien both suggest that that is due to the dying of the genre, not the innate fitness of children and fairy tales for one another. What we share with children isn't necessarily childish; sometimes what we outgrow is too important to be outgrown, like an ability to marvel at butterflies and sunsets, and to tremble at the footsteps of approaching giants.

Often the hero(ine) of a fairy tale is the "underdog": the virtuous but ugly girl, the stepchild, the youngest child. Children can relate to that sense of weakness. The child identifies with the character who arouses his sense of sympathy or identification, not necessarily the character who is good, but in fairy tales the hero *is* good. Fairy tales nearly always present characters who are all good or all bad, nothing in between. (The book-length Narnia tales allow more complexity than that. Even Lucy is sometimes disobedient, and Edmund and Eustace are redeemed.)

A Different Sort of Catastrophe

In Tolkien's essay "On Fairy-Stories," he says that it is natural for humans to create fantasy. Being made in the image of a Creator, God, we are subcreators. As in fairy tales, life is dangerous, wild, and unpredictable. Tolkien coined a term for the sudden joyous turn toward the happy ending, the fleeting glimpse of joy as the heroes win the day, instead of the catastrophe we are expecting; he called it a "eucatastrophe." Just when all seems lost, virtue wins. The same is true in the greatest story, the story of Jesus, and all good stories (including Narnia). Even in *The Last Battle*, when all hope really is lost in Narnia, the eucatastrophe takes those who love Aslan to a new Narnia, Aslan's own country.

Fairy Tales Get Better with (Our) Age

Lewis, and Tolkien as well, felt that books that only appeal to children are poor books and probably less attractive to children than books that can also appeal to adults. It's no surprise, then, that *The Chronicles of Narnia* are as attractive to adults as to children. Adults can legitimately read fairy tales as a branch of literature, not as a sign of immaturity.

Lewis admitted that he liked fairy tales better as an adult because he came to them with a deeper grasp of the world than he had as a child.

He says that the adult who can still enjoy fairy tales has been able to keep some pleasures of childhood and added adult pleasures as well—a pretty good deal.

Because we do not always think and respond as we should, we need a guide to tell us what is proper. Lewis points out that one of the best ways to train ourselves in good is to practice and to imagine doing and being what is good. Children play at being grown-up, and they play at being brave. It is valuable for them to become familiar with literature that trains their imagination in what is good and true. In reading good literature, we identify with people who are further along the path to mercy, courage, and other virtues that we long to possess in greater measure. And by falling in love with goodness and holiness, whether in human characters, Aslan, or Jesus Christ Himself, we come closer to the goodness we long for.

Narnia—Where Fairy Tales Come to Life

Lewis seems to enjoy throwing imaginary creatures into Narnia, sometimes for the sheer joy of including them. In *Voyage*, only Lucy and Reepicheep see an underwater city of merpeople, and the captain strictly warns them not to tell the others, lest men jump overboard and desert the ship. Lewis invented one creature, the gloomy but loyal Marsh-wiggle, for *Chair*.

Lewis believed talking beasts could in some ways convey human traits better than people could; being simpler, an animal can convey one particular characteristic (like the Badger's stubborn loyalty in *Caspian*). Nobody expects fairy tales to convey real life, but they can show life's *essence* better than realistic stories can. For one thing, the fairy tale takes the reader out of himself, beyond his own experiences, in a way that realistic stories cannot, according to Lewis. Serious stories represent one specific time and place, one specific dilemma at a time. Fairy tales represent the bigger human choices to do good or evil, to keep promises or not.

Children cannot be shielded from all real dangers, but life's dangers can often be met better by the child who has learned courage through identifying with dragon-slaying knights. Fairy tales show that good can overcome evil, they clarify the difference, and they help readers *want* to be on the side of good. Meeting Aslan in Narnia can help readers in the real world want to be good.

Lewis Gets Medieval on Us

Lewis was a scholar on medieval and Renaissance times and literature. Clearly, it was a time period he enjoyed. Lewis was a self-avowed dinosaur, who felt like he very nearly *was* a citizen of the Middle Ages.

Lewis heartily disliked the twentieth-century sense that truth was not the issue; being up-to-date and "modern" was more important. He claimed that our age was a day of ghosts and dwarfs—halfway-developed people with little moral depth. In his writing, he had a chance to woo people toward a taste for a fuller, more developed humanity.

Taking the Evil Out of Medieval

The word *medieval* refers to the Middle Ages—a period of European history from about A.D. 500 to about A.D. 1500. The *Chronicles* have many elements of medieval times (even an occasional dragon). In reading them, it's helpful to know a bit of how medieval people looked at reading and storytelling, the heavens and religious things, and science and ways of understanding the world. (Notes in this section are based on Lewis's book *The Discarded Image*.)

A Deep Love of Language

In the Middle Ages, literacy was rarer than today, and, of course, books were much rarer. But the age had a bookish character, and literature was very important. Medieval people had a high view of authority, and an author's authority was unquestioned (even outside his expertise, so a poet's work might be cited as an expert opinion on farming).

Medieval chronicles and legends were about people more than about social conditions. Medieval authors did not feel their own age to be very admirable, but when they wrote about other ages, their writings lacked a sense of being about a different period. One would think, from their writings, that people of all times and places dressed the way they themselves did and ate the way they did.

Magic and Myth

For a good, generally readable introduction to the medieval period, see Lewis's book *The Discarded Image* (Cambridge Univ. Press, 1964). This book's description of the medieval understanding of the heavens and of literature gives greater depth to the *Chronicles* and much of Lewis's other fiction, especially his Space Trilogy.

The Big Picture

The Middle Ages were nothing if not ordered. Its people were not dreamers, as the ballads might suggest, but organized people with systems for everything. (The ballads and romances were entertainment outside their normal way of looking at the world.) From Aquinas's *Summa Theologica* to Dante's *The Divine Comedy*, we can see some of these systems. Even war was heavily formalized, being fought according to the arts of heraldry and rules of chivalry (as in the *Chronicles*).

Their proudest achievement was the Model of the Universe, which systemized all of creation and which was not finally abandoned until the late seventeenth century. Medieval people had a true delight in the universe, believing it to be meaningful. Their love of nature was spontaneous and deep. Their literature was considered more interesting if it hearkened back to the model; Lewis admits that their literature could be rather dry because they believed everything to be so interesting that they made no special effort to make it so.

A Living Universe

Planets and other heavenly bodies played a significant role in medieval thought. All the heavenly bodies were thought to rotate around Earth. (The universe was believed to be a perfect sphere.) Each celestial body was guided in its movement by a heavenly being, a god. Each planet was named for a god, was controlled by that god, and, in theory, was used interchangeably with that god. Earth itself didn't need one because they believed it doesn't move. (Dante, however, assigns Fortune as Earth's chaperone.) Also each heavenly body was associated with a metal: for example, Sol (the sun) with gold, Mars with iron, Mercury with quicksilver (which we usually call *mercury*), Venus with copper, and the moon with silver.

Many of the *Chronicles* show Narnian stars singing or communicating with one another and with Narnians. (The creation scene in *Nephew* may be the most famous, but stars as personal beings are mentioned in at least four of the *Chronicles*.) At the end of Narnia, in *Battle*, Aslan even calls all the star people home to the new Narnia.

Of Angels and Gods

Plato and his adherents saw angels as having bodies. The thought in the Middle Ages was that two things or beings could not meet by themselves, but needed a third force to bring them together. Angels, for instance, were necessary to bridge the gap between God and people. (That isn't far from the biblical picture in one sense because man's sin makes it necessary for Jesus to take our punishment and "bridge the gap" between God and man. But from a Christian perspective, angels cannot take that particular role; they act only as God's messengers.) While Dante's angels were majestic, Milton's angels were more like the physical gods of Homer and Virgil.

The Middle Ages knew Earth was a globe but hadn't yet figured out a way to represent that on a map, so they showed only our own hemisphere. Maps, however, were inaccurate and intended as artistic representations of Earth rather than for practical use in navigation.

An Old Way of Writing New Things

Lewis wrote in the twentieth century, but he didn't feel like he was a real part of it. Narnia itself is more medieval than modern. From its sky of singing stars to its talking beasts, chivalrous mice, and code of honor, Narnia takes us out of our everyday life into a world where the universe is big again, and where creatures large and small, including humans, are important and not mere machines and consumers.

A Tale Within a Tale: Storytelling in Narnia

Narnian history is fairly well preserved. More than a thousand years go by between the first and second visits of the Pevensie children, and in that time period, the talking animals and dwarfs go into hiding and the trees lose their voices. Yet the stories of Old Narnia, including its creation and the reign of the Pevensies, is remembered and told in secret. The stories are important, so they are kept alive, much like a culture's myths.

At the end of *Wardrobe*, it seems that only Lucy and Susan know of Aslan's great sacrifice, his death for Edmund. It seems best to them not to tell Edmund. Yet in *Caspian*, the broken Stone Table has been covered and turned into Aslan's How because of the great value of that sacrifice. Somehow the story has become known and treasured.

Lesser tales are treasured as well, from the story of "the horse and his boy" (told in its own book) to the story of why the Lone Islands became Narnian possessions (a tale unknown to King Caspian in *Voyage*, but told briefly in *Battle*). And it's a good thing for us, the readers, that the entire history of Narnia made it into print in the *Chronicles*.

The Least You Need to Know

- Fairy tales and myths have more in them than meets the eye, and so does Lewis's fairy-tale world, Narnia.

- Myths are an ancient story form that look at important life issues, including birth and death, our relation to the supernatural world, creation, and good and evil.

- Much of Narnia is infused with understandings from the medieval time period, which was Lewis's special area of study.

- Fairy tales are less serious than myths, but they are also a way of understanding the world, our place in it, and the way we should relate to other people.

Chapter 3

The Moral of the Stories: What (and How) Lewis Is Trying to Teach Us

In This Chapter

- How stories help readers understand and love what is good
- Some elements that make a book good or bad
- The Narnia books as a corrective to the wrong sort of books
- Some truths Lewis teaches

Lewis didn't like books that pounded a reader over the head with an obvious moral and a bad story. He helps us learn to love true goodness by coming to know and love good people—and hints of a world beyond—through story.

Lewis also didn't set out to make the Narnia tales be "Christian stories." He told stories from a Christian framework or worldview. He wrote the books with characters who were good or bad, in a world where the evil or good of their choices was magnified. Those stories ended up telling truths about the real world.

Lewis's Thoughts on Good and Bad Books

Lewis was an avid reader, fluent in several languages. Most of us wouldn't be able to keep up with him. But we can look to him for good suggestions about what to read—and how to read it.

The Wrong Sort of Books

Lewis was quite concerned about books that only "debunk" one's beliefs and feelings, or that try to undermine appreciation for beauty and truth. He particularly disliked doing this to our young people. In the lectures collected into his short book *The Abolition of Man*, he argues that we cannot discard "ought" (the right thing to do) and replace it only with "want" (what a person desires to do).

A child doesn't necessarily desire what is good. If he makes all his own choices, he may choose what is very bad for him (like Edmund's choice to eat several pounds of magical Turkish Delight in *Wardrobe* and then to whine for more). But when we tell children only "This is bad" and never say "This is good," we train skeptics, not young people who have discernment. To be discerning, we must know what is bad, what is good—and *why*.

Teaching children—or adults, for that matter—is more than instilling knowledge. According to Lewis, teachers are not just teaching facts; they are also training the emotions. Because a person will not always choose what is good, teachers, parents, and authors must tutor their audiences in appropriate responses. It's more than manners, but it includes manners. (Perhaps that is why Lewis's villains—notably, Edmund before his repentance—are often so very rude.)

If we want honorable citizens, we must train children to recognize honorable actions and to choose to do them. Lewis said, memorably, that we cannot make a joke of honor and then act shocked to find we have traitors in our midst. We have trained the traitors ourselves.

So what is the wrong sort of book? Obviously, this includes books that teach error or that praise evil. But we think Lewis would also include books that teach truth in a boring or *didactic* way rather than engaging the student in a desire to learn. His tongue-in-cheek mention

> **Narnian Dictionary**
>
> To say a book or a lecture is **didactic** means that it teaches a lot of information, but in a self-conscious, moralistic, and tedious fashion.

of one of Caspian's textbooks provides a good example, for its author is Pulverulentus Siccus (such a name is a strong hint Lewis doesn't like the man), and the book's title is the nauseatingly sentimental *Grammatical Garden or the Arbour of Accidence pleasantlie open'd to Tender Wits*. Lewis complained that textbooks come across as too self-assured and oversimplified—history condensed into a formula. He wanted students to wrestle with truth and not have it predigested into bland baby food. (Yuck!)

How to Turn a Dragon Back into a Boy

Eustace had read the wrong sort of books and attended the wrong sort of school. His heart had grown into the wrong sort, too, by the time we meet him in *Voyage*. Is it too late for him?

Eustace is a perfect example of a young person who is childish without being childlike, who has been trained badly and thus has begun to mature in the wrong sorts of ways. Eustace lacks the ability to empathize with others. Lewis believed empathy can be strengthened as we read fiction and learn to see the world through another's eyes.

Eustace learns empathy in *Voyage* by quite literally seeing the world through another's eyes—the eyes of a dragon. He has chosen isolation, so being turned into a dragon means he is doomed to spend days alone. He is greedy, so he becomes a member of a species known for its greed. He is lazy and does not contribute to the good of the others, so he is removed from their company until he sees how much he needs them— and how much they, in turn, need him.

Once Eustace has learned empathy, it is time for a transformation, but not transformation back into the old Eustace. When he meets Aslan, he has an opportunity to become a brand-new boy.

Magic and Myth

Dragons' habits have been documented in numerous reliable sources. They fill their dens with everything they can find of value of the precious-metal-and-gems sort. They are carnivores and usually live in caves far from others of their kind. ("Kill or be killed" is the dragons' motto.) Many breathe fire, and adult dragons can fly. In short, they do not make good pets, or good shipmates.

In *The Weight of Glory*, Lewis points out that spells are for breaking enchantments, not just inducing them. He says we are under the evil enchantments of our material world. Narnia can help us break those spells—like Puddleglum in *Chair*, stamping out the Witch's enchanted fire though it meant burning his feet. Eustace needed to be awakened from the spell of his self-obsession, and enchantment was the perfect way to do it. Perhaps Narnia's readers can be spared the need to be turned into dragons themselves by reading about the danger and taking heed.

The Right Sort of Reader

Of course, if we are good readers, we don't go to a book with our own presuppositions to make the author say what we want him to say, or dismiss his arguments before we've heard them.

In a letter to his friend Arthur Greeves, Lewis said he thought that it was worth putting in some effort to get the most out of a book. He listed some of the things he himself had done when reading a book: draw maps of its geography, put in running headlines, underline, and then create an index for anything he had underlined.

He recommended firsthand sources as better, and often easier to read, than secondary sources that try to explain them. He commented that the more up-to-date a book is, the sooner it will be dated.

Lewis loved words and could appreciate a good wordsmith even if he didn't really like a given book. (One instruction he gave to young writers was to write for the ear, not the eye. A sentence must *sound* nice. His own ear was quick to appreciate other writers who did this.) He believed there were several possible reasons one might read a book, among them the seeking of knowledge and the pursuit of beauty. (He didn't think that reading a book to impress other people was a very good reason.)

The Right Sort of Books

Lewis said that an adult can also read a good children's book with pleasure. While even the best-written book might lose its charm with the seventieth repetition of "Read this one, Mom!" a good children's book is simply a good book. We almost forget *The Chronicles of Narnia* are children's books, don't we? Or maybe we ourselves become children when we read them.

A book must find one in the right mood. The best books also lend themselves to multiple readings, according to Lewis, and good readers reread their favorite books multiple times. Lewis said the first time through, you really don't get the best parts of the reading experience, and the best books need to be reread at least once a decade.

Lewis also strongly urged readers to read books from a previous generation of authors. All generations have their own blind spots, but we can recognize the blind spots of another generation easier than we can see our own. Because we can't read books written in the future, the best correctives to our own age's blind spots is to read books written in the past. We tend, instead, to hold ourselves superior to an earlier age's blind spots and not see their correctives to our own. Lewis would say that is our ignorance, not our superiority.

Learning What Isn't Taught in School

Lewis didn't like school. That may be surprising, because he was brilliant and well educated, and was a professor his entire adult life. He didn't like the bullying that is often a part of school life for less socially adept children (including himself as a child). And he thought schools often taught in the wrong ways and focused on the wrong teachings.

So what might Lewis teach in his books that *isn't* taught in schools?

Logic and Philosophy

In *Wardrobe*, Professor Kirke is based on Lewis's tutor, William T. Kirkpatrick, who deplored shallow thinking and meaningless conversation. Two or three times in *Wardrobe*, Kirke mutters to himself, "What do they teach in those schools?" He was amazed at the reasoning skills (or lack of them) that he saw in the Pevensie children. One suspects that Lewis (and Kirkpatrick) might be even more concerned today.

In *Battle*, Kirke once again was shocked at the Pevensies not grasping a point that he found clearly stated in Plato. (Okay, don't close the book just yet. We won't try to explain Plato, honest.)

Lewis saw himself as a throwback to an earlier age that valued different things. Many of his books make carefully reasoned arguments, but he understood that Western culture was losing the ability to follow a logical argument. He argued that good philosophy must exist to counter bad philosophy.

Some of Lewis's concern goes even deeper—that schools have gotten so sidetracked by modern experiments in education that they fail to teach even the basics. Thus, his characters Eustace Scrubb and Jill Pole are enrolled in a school named Experiment House, which does many things Lewis disapproves of: children at school are allowed to do whatever they like, and many of them happen to like bullying. Bullies are seen as "interesting psychological cases" for the adults to talk with. The adults get to know the bullies pretty well, and they even learn to like them more than they like the other children. Students in Experiment House don't learn much French or math, but they do learn about getting away from bullies.

Today the whole idea of objective truth is being undermined in Western culture, as is the idea that teachers are supposed to teach. (In much of educational philosophy, teaching has been replaced with "facilitating," which is often a fancy way of saying that students know more than teachers do. Lewis would have despised this notion.)

Navigating Narnia

When the Society for the Prevention of Progress made Lewis a member, he wrote a hearty acceptance of the honor in May 1944. He promised to continue his "unremitting practice of Reaction, Obstruction and Stagnation." He was being funny, of course. But he never cared whether he was in style.

Reading for Pleasure

I (Cheryl) have known college graduates who have read only one book in their entire lives that wasn't assigned reading, and I have interacted with educated professionals who haven't read a book for pleasure in several years. Lewis wouldn't have had any sympathy for or understanding of such a mind-set.

But isn't reading for pleasure a luxury? Lewis would argue that good books form our thought life and also our character. Good books can make us more interesting and more compassionate. Of course, it matters very much that we like *good* books.

In *Screwtape Proposes a Toast* (an addition to *The Screwtape Letters*), Screwtape speaks of the importance of getting rid of all human excellence, whether moral, cultural, social, or intellectual. If society makes sure that excellence is not praised, mediocrity can become the norm. Of course, as always where Screwtape is involved, Lewis was really suggesting the opposite: in this case, humans must seek the excellent and value the excellent. Finding pleasure in the good, including good books, makes one a fuller human being.

How Lewis Tries to Teach Us

In his more than 30 books, Lewis used many teaching methods. His nonfiction essays argued logically from one truth to another. In his fiction, especially the *Chronicles*, he woos. He is training the imagination and the emotions to love what is good. The reader can see why Lucy's generous, loving trust wins her friends and why Eustace's endless whining might cause others to get tired of him. As we grow to love Aslan, we, too, are open to his instructions and his warnings.

Lewis uses humor and hyperbole (exaggeration for the sake of effect) to make his points as well. Eustace has no redeeming qualities when we meet him; he is *thoroughly* nasty until after he meets Aslan. Exaggeration? Yes—even the third-grade bully has *some* good traits. (Well, come to think of it, he even dressed weird. Maybe he *didn't* have any good characteristics.) But through the exaggeration, we get the point.

This *Isn't* Sunday School

Lewis was concerned that sometimes we can do the right thing, but not because we want to do so. He spoke in *Letters to Children* of duty substituting for desire. When we plod along doing the right thing, but without our hearts in it, we are in danger of being wooed away to a more exciting wrong choice. We think we're doing the right thing, but it isn't because we *love* the good. (It might be because we're afraid of getting caught.) But he also saw the necessity of doing the right thing because it was the right thing, even if at the moment the heart doesn't respond.

Children raised in church soon learn the proper "Sunday school answer" for questions, and they can give that answer to adults. But too often, their minds and hearts are a million miles away. They're bored by the Sunday school answers, even the huge and magnificent ones, through overfamiliarity. In Aslan, Lewis is able to sneak past Sunday-school boredom to show us Jesus all over again, and show us our duty in the guise of stories that provide examples of how duty is *good* and desirable. Lewis said a perfect person would never act out of mere duty because he'd always *want* to do the right thing.

When good becomes mere duty, not our desire, we also miss much of the pleasure of a life well lived. If our goodness is just following rules that we don't really like, we can steal much of the joy from our family, friends, and even God. Lewis wanted to awaken his reader to seeing the beauty of the world in which we live and the goodness of the way it functions. He wanted readers to be able to take delight in simple pleasures: good food, beautiful scenery, and pleasant conversation. He wanted us to see that the world God made really is a good world.

Lewis thought that we make a mistake when we try to separate emotion and the intellect. We can't really engage a person's thought processes without engaging the person's heart. For any long-term learning to take place, we must care about what we study. The heart, not just the head, must be convinced. Morality itself isn't enough without *love* of the good. Lewis's *worldview* included the idea that the good can be discovered and that the good is beautiful, not drudgery.

Lewis's first attempt at fiction was *Pilgrim's Regress.* Many people see it as one of his less successful books, but in it he explored the idea of proper longings. In *Regress*, the young hero, John, was drawn to pictures of a beautiful island and simply had to try to find it. Pictures (even word pictures) move us; lists of facts or rules usually don't. And what is Narnia but a series of well-drawn pictures?

> ### Narnian Dictionary
>
> A person's **worldview** is the totality of thoughts that make up his major philosophy about the world, whether conscious or unconscious. Worldview includes one's beliefs about God, human relationships, the purpose of life, morality, what is true, and how one discovers truth. Lewis's worldview was that of a Christian whose beliefs are based on the Bible.

A Story, Not a Lecture

We tend to put up our defenses when someone tells us what we *ought* to do. (Lewis would point out that this is our inherent bias toward doing things our own way rather than being willing to be under authority— our sin nature.) We resist being told what to do even if we already know we should do what the person is telling us. Stories *show* us instead of telling us; they win us over to the author's way of seeing the world—whether the author's lessons are good or bad. At least temporarily, we see the world the way the author does by seeing it through his eyes.

Navigating Narnia

Early children's books were moral lessons for children. In Aesop's fables, the brief story was told as a sweetener to help the lesson go down easier. In books like *Little Women*, the author periodically stops telling the story to give a moral lesson. Lewis knew that the reader's brain shuts down until the story starts up again, and he kept the story moving.

One of the first rules for anyone serious about writing is "Show, don't tell." In other words, don't tell the reader "Eustace annoyed everyone"; show Eustace being annoying, and let us figure out for ourselves "Wow, that boy is obnoxious." The same principle can be applied in a slightly different way, one that Lewis learned well: show the reader why virtue pays and vice does not; don't stop the story by inserting moral points.

For Goodness' Sake!

A regular temptation for characters in the *Chronicles*—and real people today—is to seek personal power instead of doing the right thing, if one must choose between them. (We aren't just talking about politicians, either, though most of them make *really* good examples of this.) Some in Narnia are perfectly willing to be on Aslan's side if his side seems to be winning. But they don't value goodness because it is *right*.

The dwarf Nikabrik never fully chooses Aslan's side (*Caspian*). When Aslan doesn't act as fast as Nikabrik would like, he investigates other possibilities and finally shows his true colors. He's willing to follow Aslan *or* the White Witch, whichever one can bring him what he really wants.

Lewis saw relativism coming into our culture quickly. Relativism is the idea that truth isn't certain, but varies depending on what you want to do with it. In other words, it might be good to be honest, but if it's more important to win an election, then lying is okay. But Lewis knew that one cannot choose bad means for good ends.

Susan was another character who was willing to follow Aslan … sort of. Her own safety was really more important, and she never followed Aslan whole-heartedly. Trivial things eventually became more important to her, and she stopped caring about Aslan or Narnia at all.

See for Yourself

In *The Chronicles of Narnia*, we are immersed in the story. Ever notice how effectively Lewis awakens each of our five senses? From magic Turkish Delight to platefuls of fine soil served for the pleasure of dryads (tree people), readers sample Narnian food. With Reepicheep, we taste the strong, sweet water from the eastern edge of the world. We smell Narnia's rainstorms, its flowers, and its caves—and the perfume of Aslan's mane.

We see the fauns dancing and the waves lapping against the *Dawn Treader*. We hear Susan's horn calling for help and Aslan's roaring challenge to the White Witch. The fur coats in the wardrobe brush against our skin as we approach Narnia. We notice when the coats give way to tree branches, and we hear and feel the crunch of snow underfoot. (And oh, how cold it has gotten!) We know the heavy feel of a sword in our inexpert hands. And we may even long to pick up Reepicheep and cuddle him, like Lucy wants to do.

We feel Jill's sense of awe-filled fear as she looks down the cliff of Aslan's country and realizes she cannot even see the bottom. We long to dance with Aslan when he comes back to life, in that romp Susan and Lucy had with him, the joyful game that felt like dancing with a thunderstorm but also like playing with a kitten.

And as we experience each of our senses coming alive, we ourselves become Narnians and lovers of Aslan. We are there when Aslan teaches, when he scolds, when he gives lion kisses. We are sad when he leaves us unexpectedly and we, like the children in the *Chronicles*, don't know when he'll be coming back. We are on Aslan's side in Narnia, and maybe we'll be on his side in our world, too.

Lessons Worth Learning

Lewis wrote *The Chronicles of Narnia* near the end of his life, and by that time he had a lot of wisdom to pass on. In these books, he tells us much of what we need to know about life and manners in the larger-than-life form of the entire history of a world. Let's look at a few of those lessons.

Respect and Courtesy

Manners are more than a surface trait. They are a way to show proper respect for another person. Two Narnian characters stand out to us as particularly courteous: Reepicheep and Peter the High King.

Reepicheep? The cheeky mouse? Yep. Reepicheep spoke his mind, but he respected authority, the rules of society, and good manners. He was quick to take offense because his small size tended to bring out others' disrespect—but he was also quick to forgive offense, and he didn't hold a grudge. He worked hard and respected hard work in others.

In *Voyage*, Reepicheep's size kept him from helping the crew when hard rowing needed to be done, so he made up for his limits by making himself useful in another way—staying up all night to guard the ship's water supply. (Eustace rather wished Reepicheep had found a better way to be useful. See, Eustace decided it was the middle of the night and it would be quite impolite to wake someone up to ask if the water rationing really applied to him. He was pretty sure it didn't. Reepicheep was pretty sure it did.)

Peter had the honor and responsibility of being High King. Sometimes that meant settling disputes among others, including other kings (Edmund and Caspian, for instance, in *Caspian*), which has to be sort of a nasty thing to do. But he took his responsibility seriously, and his wisdom and confidence forced others to respect him and accept his authority.

Seeing and Believing

In Narnia, it is sometimes hard to believe everything you hear. Many have a hard time believing in the truth of a talking lion who hasn't been seen around these parts for, oh, a few hundred years. By Caspian's day, no one had seen a talking lion, or even a talking badger or dwarf, in ages. The creatures of Old Narnia had to come out of hiding before the rest of Narnia started believing again.

What about those who do see truth but won't believe? They are the real fools. Whether the dwarfs in *Battle*, Uncle Andrew in *Nephew*, or the Dufflepuds in *Voyage* who simply refuse to believe that their caretaker has their best interest at heart, unbelief hurts oneself as well as others. Fortunately, Lewis also shows us what happens when determined unbelief finally gives way to trust—as when Eustace finally meets Aslan in *Voyage* and realizes he has been a fool before he is fully confirmed in that role.

Reputation Matters

In crises, when the proper course might be a matter of honest dispute, it helps to know ahead of time who is a more trustworthy leader. Whether one is keeping promises to friends or working hard when others are shirking their duties, reputations are built in everyday life and tested in times of crisis.

Who would you trust in a pinch: Eustace or Reepicheep? If Edmund says Narnia is make-believe and Lucy says it is real, whom do you believe? Who usually tells the truth? Whose integrity is worth risking your life?

Children easily form habits of shifting blame onto others, exaggerating, or outright lying. Lewis shows us throughout the *Chronicles* that our daily choices affect others, and they affect whether others trust us when it counts.

We Can't Stay the Same

It's easy to drift through life and to put off real change for some other time. Lewis wants to wake us up. We need to choose: truth or error. Habits that lead to life, or habits that follow death. He makes us understand the necessity to really see ourselves and be changed.

In *Nephew*, Uncle Andrew chooses blindness. Face to face with Aslan, he shuts his ears and eyes. It is a grave loss for him. Jadis actually sees the truth. She can't close her eyes to it. But she actively flees. Strawberry, Digory, Polly, and cabby Frank see Aslan and choose him.

One group of characters does in fact stay the same without negative consequences: the honest talking beasts. Trufflehunter the badger in *Caspian* regularly repeats his reason for believing in Aslan and trusting him even in trying times: "We're beasts, and we don't change." Having never chosen selfishness, they do not need to repent.

Childlike vs. Grown-Up

The best way to compare the positive trait of childlikeness with a false maturity is to look at sisters Lucy and Susan. Lucy is the youngest of the Pevensie siblings and also the one who loves Aslan the most. She is inclined to give others the benefit of the doubt. Her gift from Father Christmas in *Wardrobe* includes a cordial of a healing liquid. It is her joy to heal others, but her loving presence heals, too. She even kissed Eustace when he was a dragon.

Lucy is innocent of evil, and her reaction to Narnia, and especially to its great ruler, is childlike awe. Her longing for Aslan overrides any other wish, and she is heartbroken when told (at the end of *Voyage*) that she won't be coming back to Narnia. She tells Aslan that Narnia isn't the biggest loss; she can't bear not to see him again. It is to Lucy that Aslan entrusts the truth that she can know him in our world, too (as Jesus Christ).

Susan is far more practical, unwilling to be swept away by her emotions—and thus unable to fully experience Narnia. She cannot let herself go and love and trust Aslan the way her little sister can. The irony is that she is not any safer for her caution, because they are in Aslan's care. Susan takes on Aslan's role in trying to keep them safe. When Lucy insists, in *Caspian*, that she must follow Aslan by herself, although the others do not see him and don't want to follow him based on Lucy's say-so, Susan resorts to being a big sister. She says Lucy is being "naughty" and insists that she is not to go off by herself.

It is a good thing to mature, to grow and learn. It is a bad thing to outgrow a childlike wonder and love, illustrated by Lucy. Before Aslan, we are all children—or should be.

The Value of a Good Friend

The last king of Narnia, Tirian (*Battle*) has a lifelong friend, Jewel, with whom he served in battles as a younger man. That Jewel is a unicorn and Tirian a man seems immaterial. They offer each other protection, counsel, companionship—even a lifetime of memories. Nothing is more valuable than a loyal friend. The *Chronicles* are loaded with friends, though some partnerships take a while to solidify: Digory Kirke and Polly Plummer, Eustace Scrubb and Jill Pole, Mr. Tumnus and Lucy, and many more.

Good friends support each other and trust each other. Eustace, Jill, Rilian, or Puddleglum would have been overcome by the Green Witch in *Chair* if any one of them had been by him- or herself. (Remember that Rilian had lived in slavery to her for several years.) But the four of them together were able to overcome her.

God Sightings

The Bible has a lot to say about human relationships, including friendship. Ecclesiastes 4:9–12 lists several ways that two people are better than one and then points out that a rope of three strands is hard to break. What are these three strands? Two friends who love each other and love God.

Look Before You Leap (to Conclusions)

Sometimes our first view of something is the wrong view and we must see beneath the surface. It might seem unwise to trust a lion. Or silly to have any confidence in the fighting abilities of a mouse, even if that mouse is, in mouse terms, a giant of 2 feet tall. If one must walk to a city of giants, does one want the world's gloomiest traveling companion?

Yet the outside appearance is rarely the most important thing. When we know the heart of a person, we can make our decisions to trust based on what really matters.

Aslan is a true beast, but he is faithful. Reepicheep is only a mouse, but his courage lends bravery to others, and his sword at an enemy's ankle can be enough to trip and destroy the enemy. And yes, one wants gloomy Puddleglum as a traveling companion. For he may believe that the danger of floods and giants makes this trek unlikely to succeed—but if you're going, he'll go with you, and he won't turn back when danger does come. It's not what we look like that matters—it's what we do.

The Least You Need to Know

- Lewis believed that a good story was an effective way to mold and teach young people.

- Lewis didn't think classroom lectures and textbooks were the most effective ways to teach.

- Lewis consciously worked to influence his readers to love good, reject evil, and know the difference between them.

Chapter 4

Putting Narnia on the Map: Exploring the Land and Its Inhabitants

In This Chapter

- An understanding of Narnia's culture and history

- A look at Narnia's relations with its neighboring lands, people from Earth, and Aslan's country

- The creatures of Narnia

Narnia is different from our world in many ways. First, one never knows where magic will show up. Time flows on a different sort of schedule; one simply cannot know how much time is passing in Narnia while one is on Earth. Animals speak. Giants and fauns and centaurs walk and talk.

Narnia has a strong cultural heritage, with a history of mostly good kings, law-abiding citizens, and a ruler who is good. The citizens are diverse but bound by their love of Aslan—as well as good food, dance, storytelling, and the value they place on friendship with one another.

The Nation of Narnia and Its Neighbors

Unless you've been to Narnia yourself, you may appreciate a few hints about the inhabitants and the country before you go. Narnia's neighboring lands don't come into the stories much, but we probably should look at them as well to be sure we understand their relationship to Narnia.

A Quick Look at Narnian Geography

Fortunately, Narnia isn't a big or complex country, so it won't take us long to mention the main points of its geography as seen on a map. The best place to start is Lantern Waste. Not only was that just beyond the wardrobe where the Pevensie children entered Narnia in *Wardrobe* (and where they exited Narnia years later), but it was the approximate location of Aslan's creation of the new land. There the lamppost grew on Narnia's first day when the Witch tried to kill Aslan. It thus has several similarities to the Garden of Eden in the Bible's book of Genesis: the place of creation, and the place where evil entered.

One of the most significant of Narnia's features is the castle from its Golden Age, Cair Paravel, where Kings Peter and Edmund and Queens Susan and Lucy reigned. Eventually, the peninsula of Cair Paravel became an island, the Telmarines avoided the area in fear of the trees that had grown up at the mouth of the river, and Cair Paravel was overgrown.

The Stone Table, reminiscent of *Stonehenge*, is a place of deep magic. The table was used for the greatest sacrifice in *Wardrobe*, the slaying of Aslan by the White Witch, and it broke in half when Aslan came back to life. After that, it was sheltered under what became Aslan's How, the setting for the battle in *Caspian*.

Narnian Dictionary

Stonehenge is an ancient group of stones in Southern England (built roughly between 3000 and 1500 B.C.), formed of large upright stones in the shape of a circle. Stone lintels cross pairs of stones, making them look rather like medieval gallows. Its use is unclear, but it has become immersed in British legend, including legends of Merlin.

Most editions of the *Chronicles* have a map of Narnia in the back of each book and a map of the specific book's territory in the front (except for *Magician's Nephew*, which doesn't have a map in the front).

Sailing in Narnia

The Great Eastern Ocean is at the edge of Narnia, east of Cair Paravel. It is mysterious and wonderful because Aslan comes from over the sea. The ocean is important on several levels. The east, the direction of sunrise, has significance in mythology and religion (e.g., the biblical Garden of Eden and the historical significance of the Middle East). Crossing a river, often the Jordan River, is an image of death in Christian literary sources, including *Pilgrim's Progress*. The sea beyond the Lone Islands was unexplored until *Voyage;* the adventure of the voyage is compelling, but the chance of sailing toward Aslan's country even more so. Eventually only Reepicheep and the human children continue east, Reepicheep sailing all the way to Aslan's country. The children meet Aslan in order to return home. Caspian reluctantly returns to Narnia with his ship, in spite of his own preference to go with Reepicheep directly to Aslan's country.

Skies over Narnia

We know very little detail about the Narnian sky, except the names of a few planets. Most significant is that the stars in Narnia are not balls of gas, but shining beings. In *Nephew*, they sing along with Aslan as they are created; in *Voyage*, we meet two or three stars (Coriakin, Ramandu, and Ramandu's daughter). In *Battle*, the stars are called home to the new Narnia.

Magic (Psst, Not All the Trees Are Friends)

Those from our land nearly always know they've experienced magic as they enter Aslan's land. The fact that they have entered at all, through a painting or a wardrobe or some other means, is a pretty good clue! Walking through Narnian woods, an unprepared visitor could be in for a nasty—or pleasant—surprise. In Narnia, the trees are awake, not just alive and rooted to the ground. And they aren't all friendly, either. Throw in a witch or two and a minor magician, and ... well, don't say we didn't warn you. Be careful.

Navigating Narnia

Narnian time is unpredictable. No time passed on Earth while the Pevensies became adults in Narnia. Only one Earth year passed between *Wardrobe* and *Caspian*—more than 1,000 years in Narnia. One year between *Voyage* and *Chair*, Earth time, was 70 in Narnia. Narnian time worked the other way once—a week on Earth in *Battle* was but minutes in Narnia.

Getting There from Here—Doors from the World of Men

The prophecy that foretold the White Witch's doom through four human kings and queens did not specify how they would enter Narnia. Thus, the very concept of doors from the world of men terrifies her. And indeed, it never is clear how one might enter Narnia, as most entrances are used only once. Quick, which *Chronicle* doesn't have any new visitors from our world? Only *The Horse and His Boy*. Let's look briefly at who has entered Narnia from our world, and which passage each one took to get there (and to return home!). We'll also see a few other books that used similar gates for their characters to enter a new world.

People	Door into Narnia	Door out of Narnia	Book	Similar Literary Use
Pevensie children (Peter, Susan, Edmund, Lucy)	Wardrobe in Professor Kirke's spare room (Lucy, then Lucy and Edmund, then all four Pevensie children).	Through the same wardrobe.	*The Lion, the Witch and the Wardrobe*	E. Nesbit, *The Aunt and Amabel*
Telmarines' ancestors	Accidentally, through a cave.	Through a wooden doorway Aslan sets up.	*Prince Caspian* (hundreds of years before *Caspian*, where the story is told)	*Ali Baba and the Forty Thieves*
Peter, Susan, Edmund, and Lucy Pevensie	Aslan pulls them into Narnia from a train going back to school.	Through a doorway Aslan sets up to send the Telmarines home.	*Prince Caspian*	E. Nesbit, *The Railway Children*
Edmund and Lucy Pevensie, Eustace Scrubb	Looking at a picture of a Narnian ship, they discover the ship is actually moving.	Aslan sends them back through a door he opens in the sky.	*Voyage of the Dawn Treader*	P. L. Travers, *Mary Poppins*

continues

continued

People	Door into Narnia	Door out of Narnia	Book	Similar Literary Use
Eustace Scrubb and Jill Pole	Through a gate in a school wall.	Aslan knocks down a school wall (he allows Caspian to get a glimpse of England), and then repairs the wall.	*The Silver Chair*	John Bunyan, *Pilgrim's Progress*
Digory Kirke, Polly Plummer, the Witch Jadis, Uncle Andrew, cabby Frank, and Frank's horse Strawberry	Through the Wood Between the Worlds, wearing magic rings made by Uncle Andrew.	Digory, Polly, and Uncle Andrew return by Aslan's power; others stay in Narnia.	*The Magician's Nephew*	Algernon Blackwoods, *The Education of Uncle Paul*
Nellie (Queen Helen)	Aslan pulls her into Narnia.	She stays in Narnia.	*The Magician's Nephew*	*Aladdin and the Magic Lamp*
Jill and Eustace	Pulled in from railway.	They stay in the new Narnia.	*The Last Battle*	J. K. Rowling, *Harry Potter and the Sorcerer's Stone*
Seven friends	Railway accident.	They stay in the new Narnia.	*The Last Battle*	*The Little Prince*

The Wood Between the Worlds

The very first connection between our world and Narnia, in *Nephew*, comes by way of a magic in-between place.

Uncle Andrew expects his magic rings to take the children (Digory and Polly) to a new world, but instead they find themselves in an "in-between" world, a quiet place of trees and small ponds. This is what one gets from wandering in other worlds without a map: the first pond they jump into (after a few false starts) leads to Charn, a land of ruins and a large red sun, where Digory awakens a witch. The Wood Between the Worlds later leads them to Narnia just as it is being created.

Of course, literature contains many settings where one must choose between entry points in a new world, from fairy tale choices of which door to open to the hallway of doors in *Alice's Adventures in Wonderland* (Lewis Carroll, 1865). But the calm peacefulness of the woods is an unexpected entry point to the chaos of dying old worlds and newly created young ones.

Beyond Narnia: Archenland and Calormen

Two other nations are close enough to Narnia to show up on its maps. The first of these is an ally, Archenland, located to the south of Narnia. In *Horse*, we see young Prince Corin from Archenland in the company of King Edmund and Queen Susan because he is Susan's friend. When Calormen's rash young Prince Rabadash attacks the small nation of Archenland, Narnia quickly comes to Archenland's aid.

The nation is not only peaceful, but good. King Lune explains to his sons that the law makes a man king, and the king must be under the law as much as anybody, as well as a servant to his entire nation. This follows the principle of *Lex rex* (the law is king), seventeenth-century theologian Samuel Rutherford's description of the limited power of government on which Western nations such as England and the United States are based. The usual system for a monarchy is *Rex lex*, the king "is" the law and has all the authority, even if his authority is unjust.

Calormen, across the desert from Archenland and farther south, is a threat to both Archenland and Narnia. In *Horse*, the threat to Archenland is repulsed because Aslan ensures that young Shasta's traveling

Navigating Narnia

Calormen is a very practical place, shown by the extreme dullness of its "poetry" (*Horse*). Arsheesh quotes a poet as saying, "Application to business is the root of prosperity, but those who ask questions that do not concern them are steering the ship of folly toward the rock of indigence." *Practical* is always a negative word when Lewis uses it; he means "uncreative and dull."

party will hear of it and will be able to warn the threatened nation and Narnia. In *Battle*, the threat comes more subtly at first, through deceit and inappropriate trade, not through warfare until it is too late to save Narnia.

Emeth in *Battle* is a Calormene; though he worships the god Tash, he willingly bows to Aslan and is allowed to enter the new Narnia. Lewis seems thus to take great care not to paint any culture or people as irredeemable or beyond hope.

The land of Telmar is far beyond the western mountains, too far distant to appear on any Narnian maps. From Telmar come the Telmarines, who appear extensively in *Caspian*. Caspian himself is a Telmarine, but otherwise we know little of Telmar.

The Humans of Narnia

Narnia initially doesn't have any human inhabitants of its own. Because all humans are descendants of Adam and Eve, Aslan chose instead to allow limited entry to Narnia from Earth. Some Narnian time periods have had many humans, and some very few.

Kings and Queens of Narnia

All real kings and queens of Narnia must be sons of Adam and daughters of Eve. (At least one queen in Narnia, the White Witch in *Wardrobe*, was a fraud and pretender to the throne because she wasn't human but acted as if she were.)

As the badger Trufflehunter put it in *Caspian*, Narnia is not man's country, but mankind should rule it.

We know only a few of the kings and queens in Narnia's history. Here are the ones we know, with parallels with people in the Bible, many of them kings and queens.

Known Kings and Queens of Narnia

Royal Persons	Known For	Story Told In	Compared to Biblical Person(s)
King Frank and Queen Helen	First king and queen of Narnia (from London).	*Nephew*	Adam and Eve (Genesis 2–3)
King Gale (ninth in descent from King Frank)	Delivered Lone Islands from a dragon.	*Battle* (story told in passing)	David (1 Samuel 17)
Queen Swanwhite (before the White Witch)	Her great beauty.	*Battle* (mentioned briefly)	Esther (Esther 2)
The White Witch	A usurper to the throne who held Narnia under 100 years of winter.	*Wardrobe*	Satan (Mark 1)
Peter the High King, Queen Susan, King Edmund, and Queen Lucy	Entered Narnia from England; delivered Narnia from the White Witch. Their rule was the Golden Age of Narnia.	*Wardrobe* (with short visits that make up several additional stories)	Jesus' disciples (Mark 14:12–26; 16)

continues

Known Kings and Queens of Narnia   *(continued)*

Royal Persons	Known For	Story Told In	Compared to Biblical Person(s)
Caspian the First (Caspian the Conqueror)	The Telmarine who conquered Narnia and drove "Old Narnia" (dwarfs, talking animals, and talking trees) into hiding.	*Caspian* (story told to Prince Caspian as history)	Nebuchadnezzar (2 Kings 24)
Miraz the Usurper	Killed his brother, the rightful King Caspian IX, and reigned in his stead.	*Caspian*	Absalom (2 Samuel 15–18)
Caspian X (Caspian Seafarer); ninth from Caspian the Conqueror; married Ramandu's daughter	Brought back Old Narnia, explored the Northern Sea, and discovered lands beyond the Lone Islands.	*Caspian*	Nehemiah (Nehemiah 2–6)
Rilian (son of Caspian X)	Was rescued from slavery to the Green Witch.	*Chair*	The nation of Israel (Exodus 11–12)
Earlian, sixth in descent from Rilian	Nothing known of him except that he was father to Tirian.	*Battle*	None
Tirian	Bravely fights a losing battle for Narnia.	*Battle*	Jeremiah (Jeremiah 38)

Most of the kings and queens we meet are good and just. The Pevensies rule during what is known later as the Golden Age of Narnia, the time in which the White Witch is overthrown and Narnia is restored. Peter, the High King, continues to function as a higher king than any other on his returns to Narnia when he meets other kings.

Another king is needed to restore Narnia from a new threat a thousand years later. Caspian X (the Tenth) discovers that he is the true king and finds that his life is in danger. He must flee to save his life, but he also must attempt to restore Narnia to the way it used to be. Narnia is to be ruled by men and women, but it is not to be *dominated* by humans. Its talking beasts and other creatures are free citizens, not slaves. They ought not to be ruled with treachery or killed.

Perhaps it is a sign of Caspian's repentance of his ancestors' deeds that he does not pass on the name of Caspian to his own son, because Caspian was the name of the one who conquered and enslaved Narnia. Caspian X's son is Rilian, not Caspian XI.

True kings and queens of Narnia were sons of Adam and daughters of Eve (humans). Their responsibilities were given by Aslan in *Nephew*, where King Frank was told he had the responsibility to rule and name the creatures, do justice among them, and protect them from their enemies. He was not to play favorites among them and was to be first in battle and last in retreat. Aslan charged the new king and queen with being just, merciful, and brave.

Magic and Myth

A great resource for beginning to explore other worlds is the encyclopedic *Dictionary of Imaginary Places*, by Alberto Manguel and Gianni Guadalupi (Harcourt Brace, 2000). Using only the information provided in books about imaginary realms, this volume gives travel-guide information on more than 1,200 lands, including Narnia and the other locations of the *Chronicles*.

Other Sons of Adam and Daughters of Eve

Many of the humans in Narnia are temporary visitors from our world. A few visitors from our world become Narnian kings and queens. The children from our world who did not become kings and queens are these: Polly Plummer and Digory Kirke, in *Nephew*, who watch Narnia's creation; Eustace Scrubb, who sails with Prince Caspian and Edmund and Lucy Pevensie and has his life changed for the better by becoming a dragon; and Jill Pole, who goes to Narnia with Eustace so that the two of them can rescue Prince Rilian, son of Caspian. Eustace and Jill also go to Narnia in the last days of the land, to rescue the final king, Tirian, from his bonds and help him prepare for battle.

Interestingly, these people appear as royalty in the new Narnia in *Battle*, perhaps an allusion to the Bible's promise about believers reigning as kings and queens with God in heaven (Revelation 22:5).

Foreigners

The largest influx of humans in Narnia's history were the Telmarines, who got in from Earth rather accidentally (as described in *Caspian*). By the beginning of *Caspian*, Telmarines are living in Narnia in large numbers. The royal family are actually Telmarines. Because the Telmarines are afraid of the trees and have no love for the talking beasts, the woods have gradually gone silent. Narnia now appears to be a land of humans and nontalking animals.

In *Battle*, the foreigners also have a hostile intent. The Calormenes have long wanted to defeat Narnia, and now they have their opportunity. Narnians are helping them because they believe it to be the will of Aslan.

Narnia's Other Residents

Now let's meet Narnia's permanent residents, the creatures made by Aslan or descended from them. They are far more diverse than Earth's mammals, birds, reptiles, insects, and fish. In fact, Narnia really shows a necessity for tolerance and mutual understanding: humans, talking animals of numerous species (with their preferences and peculiarities), and beings from dwarfs to giants all have to come together in one community.

Talking Beasts

We make a mistake if we picture Narnian talking animals as pets who can carry on conversation. Talking beasts are given greater intelligence, the smaller species are larger in size than ordinary animals of their species, and, most important, talking beasts in Narnia are free citizens. For instance, nobody rides talking horses (except in battle).

On the day of creation, Aslan tells his creatures, "I give you yourselves." They are free to be who they were meant to be. Talking beasts retain their animal traits and personalities. Moles love to dig (it is they who plant the apple orchard at Cair Paravel during the reign of the Pevensies), dogs are optimistic and devoted, and squirrels bound through trees chattering and collecting nuts.

> **Navigating Narnia**
> Many Narnian names fit well with the personality or characteristics of the creature. Some of our favorites are Trufflehunter the badger, Pattertwig the squirrel, Glimfeather the owl, Stonefoot the giant, and Clodsley Shovel, a mole. And who can forget the Bulgy Bears in *Caspian*, complete with one thumb-sucking bruin?

Like ordinary beavers, our friends the Narnian talking beavers have built a dam and a lodge. Yet the Beavers' lodge, seen in *Wardrobe*, looks very unlike a normal beaver lodge inside. Mrs. Beaver has a sewing machine, and their home has furniture. Mr. Beaver catches fish and drinks beer.

Speech is a gift to talking beasts, and it can be lost. We see its loss numerous times in Narnia: for example, the lapsed talking bear in *Horse* that has become dangerous, and Ginger in *Battle*, who loses his speech while we watch. The enchanted dragon that was Eustace cannot speak. By the time of *Caspian*, the presence of talking beasts, dwarfs, unicorns, and talking trees is believed to be a mere myth. Most of the beasts have returned to silence, as have the woods. Fully alive Narnia has become "Old Narnia," a mere myth. Much of Caspian's task is to awaken Old Narnia and allow it to thrive again. (Note that Lewis disliked the idea that *old* automatically means inferior. In this instance, old, wild, and free is notably better than "new" and restrained, under bondage to Telmarine conquerors.)

Some of the most important talking beasts in Narnia's history include Mr. and Mrs. Beaver, who escorted three of the Pevensie children safely to Aslan at the Stone Table (Edmund wasn't with them because he had deserted to the White Witch); Reepicheep the mouse, whose courage inspires others, including much larger animals and people; and horses Bree and Hwin, whose speed delivers a message that alerts Narnia and Archenland of an approaching enemy. Puzzle the donkey, Shift the ape, and Ginger the cat play very negative roles in the closing days of Narnia, although Puzzle is trying to do what is right.

Fauns, Centaurs, and Other Such Creatures

Many of Narnia's creatures are taken from mythology and fairy tales, though Lewis tends to give them their own vivid personalities. The faun of mythology becomes the unforgettable Mr. Tumnus, Lucy's friend (you almost forget he ever had bad intentions, as he is redeemed by Lucy's love, trust, and forgiveness). By the way, fauns and satyrs are really the same being, although Lewis consistently includes both in lists of Narnian residents. (A faun is a gentler Roman version of the Greek satyr.)

Among the more noble of the Narnian creatures is the centaur (half-horse, half-man). By profession, they are stargazers and prophets, and they are honorable folk. Riding them is a rare and great honor.

Merpeople or sea people appear in two books: merpeople similar to Hans Christian Anderson's characters in *The Little Mermaid* sing at the coronation of the Pevensies in *Wardrobe*, and in *Voyage*, Lucy sees a whole undersea city of more warlike sea people.

Underneath Narnia, seen in *Chair*, are goblins who seem to be a dangerous army but turn out to be harmless, enslaved by the Green Witch, in contrast to the dangerous goblins in *The Lord of the Rings* and MacDonald's *The Princess and the Goblin*.

Probably the only creature actually invented for Narnia was the Marsh-wiggle, of whom we meet only one, Puddleglum, in *Chair*. Puddleglum is a consistent pessimist, always predicting wars and famines and vivid means of death, but he is one of Narnia's most loyal creatures. And when it counts, he is even encouraging. Although the Marsh-wiggle seems to be Lewis's own invention, the character was based on Lewis's gardener, Fred Paxton, and the name "Puddleglum" seems to have come from the line in Gavin Douglas's 1513 translation of *The Aeneid*, in which Aeneas descends to Avernus "through Stygian puddle glum."

Unity from Diversity

We get a hint of how hard it might be to rule such diverse creatures in *Caspian*, as Caspian and the creatures of Old Narnia get together for a council to determine their plans (which probably entail war with Caspian's uncle, Miraz, usurper of Caspian's throne). Every creature has a different idea of whether eating, fighting, dancing, or planning should take precedence. For Caspian, who had dealt only with humans until a few days before, the scene must have been a bit overwhelming, as it might be for you and me.

The creation scene is nearly as chaotic, and equally joyful, with animals discovering who they are. In *Chair*, the nighttime parliament of owls makes Eustace and Jill a bit suspicious: if the owls aren't plotting against the king, why don't they meet in the daytime? The owls explain: meeting in daylight means meeting under a shockingly bright sun, when any owl can hardly think straight.

To come against Narnia in war demands knowing your enemy. If good giants are aligned with the Narnians, beware. Their size and their clubs can wipe out a good number of any army quickly (although they aren't all that bright, which impedes their war strategy a great deal). And to fight a unicorn really means taking one's life in one's hands: unicorns fight by rearing onto their hind legs, then coming down on an enemy with teeth and horn and front hooves.

Talking animals are, after all, just animals who are more themselves than they were without speech. It is when animals decide to be someone else that everyone is in trouble. The ape Shift was a lazy, bossy friend to the loyal donkey Puzzle—but when Shift put on clothes and pretended to be human, all of Narnia was in for sorrow and pain. And the good donkey Puzzle was hoodwinked into pretending to be someone he was not: Aslan himself.

Evil Beings

Not all the creatures in Narnia are good. Various books record ghouls and ogres, hags and wraiths, and many other creatures whose very names are horrible. The beginning of these species is not recorded. They could have come in from outside Narnia; some of them could be good Narnian species gone bad. Clearly, they were not part of the original creation in Narnia, but they are enemies that must be dealt with.

Many of the giants in Narnia are now dangerous enemies as well. Giants were among the original creation, and some of them are still kind and gentle.

Trees That Talk

At the very beginning of creation, Aslan chose to give his trees a greater life than Earth trees have. His trees have dryads and hamadryads and silvans, basically tree spirits that are free to leave their rooted trees and walk about (although, in *Caspian*, we learn that dryads don't walk *on* the ground as we do; they wade through it).

Caspian gives us the best look at these folks. When the tale begins, the trees have been "asleep" for hundreds of years. They are still alive like any Earth tree, but their tree spirits stay in their trees. It is the Telmarines that have been unfriendly, and the trees, in their turn, are initially unfriendly to Caspian, a Telmarine.

Aslan arrives, and they revive. Lucy sees them struggling to come awake. Later, awake for the first time in hundreds of years, the trees surround Aslan. Each has its own recognizable form: pale birch girls, willow women with long hair, dignified beech women, shaggy oak men, holly men and women (the women with bright holly berries)—tree people key to Celtic mythology and to much of Faerie, including the tales of George MacDonald. As they bow and curtsy around Aslan, Bacchus, the Roman god of wine, joins them.

Because of the Telmarines' superstitious fear of the trees, the trees themselves can form a big part of the battle strategy. Certainly, the idea of a Narnia alive with talking trees and beasts does not appeal to the older Telmarines, although many of the younger ones choose to stay and take a more humble place in a restored Narnia when Aslan gives them the option.

Common Critters

In Narnia's beginning, Aslan chose some animals to be talking beasts—a male and female of each of the numerous species. He didn't choose every species, or all the animals within any selected species. Those selected to be talking beasts received a special dignity—and the responsibility to watch over the animals that were not so chosen.

One of the best indicators of people's character in Narnia is their compassion to beasts. The White Witch in *Wardrobe* is cruel to her own reindeer, and she readily turns creatures of all sorts into stone. The last king of Narnia, Tirian, is gentle to the talking beasts and the common animals as well.

God Sightings

In the very beginning of our world, Adam and Eve were given much the same charge as King Frank and Queen Helen. God told them to be fruitful and multiply, to till the ground, and to care for the land and its creatures. Adam even got to name the animals, as did King Frank. The animals are under us in authority, but how we treat them is important.

The Culture of Narnia

Humans are usually brought from our world in times of great distress in Narnia, so we see more battles, coronations, and celebrations than one might see in an average weekend in Narnia. We have only glimpses of everyday life, but quite a few looks at how Narnia fights and how it parties.

Music and Dance

A world that came to life through song (Aslan's singing in *Nephew*) might be expected to value music and dance.

One of the most original dances is seen at the end of *Chair*, when Jill pokes her head out of a cave just in time to be hit in the face with a snowball. It turns out that Narnian tradition includes a great snow dance on the first moonlit snowy night. In *The Snow Queen* by Hans Christian Andersen, the characters Gerda and Kay dance on the ice as Kay spells the word "eternity" and is thus freed from the queen's clutches. The dance in *Chair* also takes place as the Witch's power over a young prince is broken, and a land is saved.

Lucy learned the power of Narnian music on her first visit to Narnia. (That was a brief visit of a few hours, before her sister and brothers got into Narnia themselves.) In the cave of the faun Tumnus, she is served a wonderful tea, and then Tumnus plays a strange little flute made of straw. Hours later, she realizes she has been enchanted by the music and has forgotten the time.

When Caspian is beginning to restore Narnia to its former freedom, it is time to celebrate before battle. No one celebrates like Narnians who can sense freedom for the first time in many years. Bacchus, Silenus, and the Maenads dance, and their dance of plenty turns into a feast for all. For everywhere their hands or feet touch brings out a portion of the feast—meats and cakes, plentiful fruits and wines.

One of Caspian's first encounters with "Old Narnia" is dancing fauns on Dancing Lawn. Moments after seeing the dance, he is compelled to join in. Fortunately, part of his education has been learning the music of Narnia, including learning to play the recorder and the theorbo (similar to a large lute).

Storytelling

Storytelling is an art in Narnia, and an important one in the friendly land to its south, Archenland. The one story in the series that takes place mostly outside the boundaries of Narnia, *The Horse and His Boy*, is a story within the Narnian story about storytelling. In it, the stallion Bree tells his stories of battle to the boy Shasta. Most notably, Aravis uses her ancestral storytelling gift to tell her story of fleeing from an undesirable arranged marriage. (Students in Calormen are trained in storytelling the way children in other lands are trained to write essays—except, Lewis says in an aside, that the stories are more interesting than the essays.)

In *Prince Caspian*, the stories of Narnia's creation and early days are not believed anymore but are still told to children. Caspian's nurse tells him the stories, and when Caspian believes them, the nurse is dismissed.

It is then up to Caspian's tutor to tell him Narnian history from the time of his ancestor, Caspian the Conqueror. (Prince Caspian is Caspian X.) All cultures have had stories of the creation of the world and of the country's own origin; perhaps Lewis was quietly commenting on his own culture's budding disbelief in biblical history and questioning of European history.

In *Silver Chair*, the story from *Horse* is told after dinner in the castle on Eustace and Jill's first night in Narnia. Later, in Underland, the knight has food and drink brought for his guests so they can partake while he tells his story—although, unfortunately, he himself has been enchanted and he cannot remember the most important parts.

Food and Drink

Have you ever been at a star-studded banquet? Those who traveled with Caspian on the *Dawn Treader* supped with a retired star and his daughter at a feast provided by Aslan, with every good food imaginable.

Hospitality is honored in Narnia. Visitors are given the best of one's stores. (A hint on squirrel etiquette that Caspian learned from his friends: if a squirrel fetches you a nut from his larder, look away as he goes to get it so that you will not see where his larder is. Larders are a squirrel's version of ATMs.)

Home life seems generally to be modeled on English traditions. As in England, people in Narnia have *tea* in the afternoon.

In a land with such a variety of creatures, one naturally meets a variety of foods. The tree people eat fine soils, Puddleglum the Marsh-wiggle makes his own eel stew, and the owl on which Jill Pole is riding even nabs a bat as a snack while they are flying.

> **Narnian Dictionary**
>
> What is this event called **tea?** In England, as in much of Europe, lunch is often the main meal. Dinner is usually late and rather light. Tea is served around 4:00 P.M. to stave off starvation until then. Tea is a snack or light meal, served with tea, of course. Narnia apparently is under the same system for meals.

Beware the hospitality of giants, however. Not only might they wish to serve you for dinner, but Puddleglum and his friends in *Chair* found out midway through a meal in the giants' castle that they'd been eating talking stag. (Killing and eating talking beasts is, of course, forbidden in Narnia.)

And beware magic food as well. Although Edmund was initially suspicious of the White Witch, she appealed to him through his appetites and gave him magic Turkish Delight, the best he had ever eaten. Mr. Beaver told Edmund's siblings later that he had been concerned about Edmund, as he had the look of one who had eaten the Witch's food.

But oh, the meals in Narnian castles are enough to make your mouth water just reading them: meats and fruits, cakes and pies, all the stuff that we humans eat, and in great abundance. (Oddly, broccoli, lima beans, parsnips, and okra are never mentioned. Lewis himself hated broccoli and once befriended a young boy by admitting it aloud in a restaurant.)

Warfare

Unfortunately, Aslan doesn't call people from our world into Narnia just to sit around and tell stories and eat and drink by the fire. Usually, they come in at times of great crisis, and that means times of war.

Narnia is at peace in its early creation, although the Witch offers a threat down the road. *Nephew* is the only book in which we do not see a Narnian battle. In *Wardrobe*, all Narnia does battle against the White Witch and her forces, and Aslan kills the White Witch. In *Horse*, a small army from Narnia goes to back up their allies in Archenland against an invading army from Calormen. And in *Battle*, the battle is against Calormen in Narnia—and unfortunately, many Narnians are fighting on the wrong side, while the dwarfs are fighting against Narnians and Calormenes alike.

In Narnia, every warrior uses the weapon he or she uses best. For many beasts, that means teeth and claws. Hawks use their talons and beaks, horses their teeth and front feet. Mice stab at the feet of the opposing army with small swords, and giants use their clubs. With each warrior using his or her best skills and best weapons, Narnia is defended. Kings are first into battle, as decreed by Aslan at the beginning.

Home Life

We see little of Narnian home life, as most scenes in the *Chronicles* take place outdoors. What we do see suggests cozy British homes, with a fire in the winter, a few books in the bookcase, and a nice chat with friends.

The Least You Need to Know

- Narnia has a rich, varied culture and takes pride in its heritage.

- The multitude of sentient life forms in Narnia, from talking animals to human beings, requires residents to have understanding, a willingness to use one's own skills for the common good, and respect.

- Human beings in Narnia all come from our world, in many different ways.

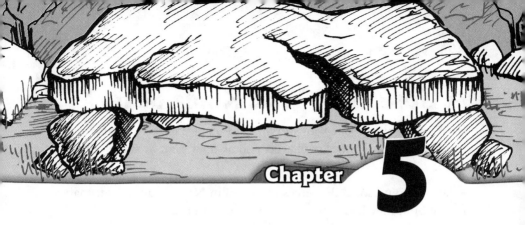

Chapter 5

Hearing Him Roar: Aslan, the Ruler of Narnia

In This Chapter

- 🌸 Aslan's place in Narnia and reasons he is a lion
- 🌸 Ways that Aslan is like—or unlike—Jesus Christ
- 🌸 Aslan's interactions with other characters

No one is neutral toward Narnia's ruler, the good lion Aslan. Those who are evil view him with suspicion, fear, or outright disbelief in his existence. Creatures who desire good long for Aslan to make one of his infrequent visits to the land he rules so wisely and well.

But the ruler of Narnia is a mystery—he comes and goes as he wishes, and pulls people in from other worlds as he wills. He is good, but he is a lion, and the wise human or animal knows Aslan is no tame kitty cat.

A Lion? Isn't That Kinda Scary?

Even in Narnia, no one wants to meet a lion face to face. Aslan, great as he is, is not "safe." He is in charge, and he does what he wants. But he is good.

Aslan is also personal. Whereas creatures in Narnia have a legitimate fear of him, they know he cares about them and their welfare. He's the king, but he laughs with them and plays with them, and he even feasts with them. So his subjects have a healthy respect of him, but they love him.

Who Is This King of the Beasts?

Aslan is the great lion who created Narnia. He is the son of the Emperor-Beyond-the-Sea. The kings and queens of Narnia rule under his authority and according to his laws. He appears in Narnia periodically, usually in times of great crisis. Sometimes several hundred years go by between his visits. He rules other lands as well, although we see that mostly indirectly. (*Horse* shows him involved in the history of Archenland.)

Aslan has great dignity, yet he does not hold himself aloof from those he rules. Aslan interacts with Narnia's kings and queens, installing them and helping them rule, but he also has time for the common folk.

Why Is Aslan a Lion?

Between Aslan's infrequent appearances in Narnia, many people and beasts tend to disbelieve he really exists at all. Those who do believe in him often start thinking that the stories are only describing Aslan's characteristics when they call him a lion. The stallion Bree is one such creature, who calls Aslan a lion but doesn't think he literally is a lion.

Of course, Aslan is a real lion. First, the King of Beasts would quite naturally be the one to rule a land of talking beasts. Lions have a dignified air that demands respect; from Aesop's fables to Disney's *The Lion King*, lions are depicted as rulers as often as owls are seen to be wise.

In addition, Aslan is based on Jesus Christ. In the Bible, Jesus is sometimes represented as a lion, but also as a lamb (as Aslan appears in one of the last scenes in *Voyage*). In one passage in the Bible's last book, Revelation, the apostle John is looking for someone who will open an important scroll. He is told that the *Lion of the Tribe of Judah* will open the scroll. He looks for the lion and sees not a lion, but a lamb (Revelation 5:6).

A lion is a great animal to represent who Aslan *is*. Aslan is solemn, yet joyful. Serious, but playful. He is strong, but gentle to his friends (like a cat with "velveted" paws). Approaching him, Narnians see the terrible and the beautiful at the same time. They know fear in his presence, but great gladness, too. Of course, a lion isn't "safe." But who needs a safe leader?

God Sightings

Why is Jesus called the **Lion of the Tribe of Judah?** Way back in Genesis, Jacob had 12 sons, whose descendants became the 12 tribes of Israel. When Jacob was dying, he gave blessings and predictions about each son and his family. Jacob called Judah a strong leader, a lion's cub, so the emblem of Judah became the lion. Jesus was born into the tribe of Judah.

The evil ones fear him without any gladness. At creation, we are told the Witch Jadis "understood" the magic in his singing as none of the others did. Yet it causes her to flee, not to approach.

Those who are wise approach in spite of their fear. Many come with their knees knocking, like the skeptical dwarf Trumpkin or the mare Hwin, who wants to go to him even if he eats her. In *Chair*, Jill is too fearful to approach, but she must draw near if she is to drink from the stream he is guarding.

Navigating Narnia

Aslan is associated with water throughout the *Chronicles*. He usually comes from over the river. In *Horse*, Shasta drinks from Aslan's paw print when it becomes a spring. In *Voyage*, as the *Dawn Treader* nears Aslan's country, the water is sweet and even satisfies hunger. And in Aslan's country, the water from the stream and Aslan's blood restore Caspian to life (*Chair*).

What We Know About Him …

Aslan is consistently the initiator in relationships with others. He chooses to interact with, protect, and lead those who cannot give him anything in return. In *Nephew*, Digory and Polly realize that they have nothing to eat on the journey to the walled garden to bring Aslan an apple to guard Narnia. They wish Aslan had arranged for their meals. The flying horse Fledge, munching the good grass, tells the children that he suspects that Aslan "likes to be asked." Like Jesus, Aslan is more than able to provide his people's needs, but he wants them to come to him and ask. He also wants them to want *him* more than they want anything they may desire to get *from* him.

Aslan is the creator of Narnia and its ultimate authority; he's personal, wise, and fun loving. He knows his creatures. When someone asks Eustace if he knows Aslan, he answers wisely, "He knows me."

Physically, he's impressive. He's brightly colored—and huge. Descriptions of his size vary; apparently, he varies in how he chooses to appear to people. Sometimes he wishes to awe people; sometimes he wants to comfort them. But often he is described as larger than an ordinary lion: taller than a horse, for instance, as big as a young elephant. His mane carries a strange but lovely perfume.

Aslan is a shrewd, wise leader. He illustrates well the truth that if people of various stations are to meet, the higher one must humble himself and come down. He is willing at times to fulfill very humble roles, including spending the night at the tombs with Shasta in the form of a large cat so that Shasta will not be frightened (*Horse*).

He delegates. He could be Narnia's one and only ruler, but instead he has set up human kings and queens. He calls children from our world to win victories he could win himself with a swipe of his paw. He rejoices in the success of his friends and is grieved when they desert him or fail to trust him.

Aslan prophesies and fulfills *prophecies*. For instance, in *Nephew*, he says that the Witch Jadis will someday cause great harm to Narnia, but he will see that the time of harm is a long time in the future and that the worst of the evil will hurt him and not others in Narnia. Obviously, he is predicting his own death at the hand of the White Witch in

Wardrobe. In *Chair*, he entrusts
Jill with four signs by which she
and Eustace will know the true
prince of Narnia. One of those
signs is that the prince will be
the first person to ask for something in Aslan's own name.

That leads us to an interesting
theological dilemma. Obviously,
Lewis had already written of
Aslan's death and coming back
to life before he ever wrote down
the prophecies regarding them.

> **Narnian Dictionary**
>
> A **prophecy** is a prediction
> about what will happen in the
> future, usually made by a prophet.
> Prophecies aren't guesses about
> what will happen; biblically they
> are supposed to come from God,
> and they should be true predic-
> tions. If a prophecy fails to come
> true, that is enough evidence that
> the one who gave it is a false
> prophet.

We are also told in *Wardrobe* about the Deep Magic, but again, Lewis
as author was behind the scenes working out the plot concerning the
Deep Magic. Is that how prophecy works in the Bible as well? Skeptics
would say it does. But check out Isaiah 53, written around 700 B.C., long
before Jesus' death on a cross in about A.D. 30, and see if the prophecy
is accurate. (That's just one example of accurate prophecy in the Bible.)

... and What We Don't

Aslan has an air of mystery about him. He chooses to reveal some
aspects of himself, and he hides others. In *Horse*, when Shasta has a
great presence walking beside him, he asks, "Who are you?" Aslan
doesn't even give his name. Instead he answers, "Myself" three times,
each time in a different tone.

Until *Battle*, we know very little about Aslan's country, where Aslan
apparently lives when he is not in Narnia. We know very little about
what he does between visits to Narnia. He is the son of the Emperor-
Beyond-the-Sea, but we know nothing at all about the Emperor (who
represents God the Father). For those left unsatisfied by little glimpses
of Aslan, a fuller picture of a perfect King is seen in the Bible—but
God Himself remains a mystery in many ways, having also chosen to
reveal only part of who He is.

How Aslan Is—and Isn't—Jesus

Aslan is based on Lewis's imagining of what it might be like if Jesus Christ appeared in a different setting and a different form. In our world, He became man. How might He appear in a world where the intelligent life is animal? Lewis never attempts to have Aslan's life in Narnia present a one-to-one correspondence with Jesus' life on Earth because he's in a different world, not a different place that's only a picture of our world.

He's in Charge

Aslan is clearly the king. He has power, authority, and wisdom. He can override the White Witch's magic (*Wardrobe*), pull people into Narnia, orchestrate circumstances, and rout his enemies. His enemies fear him, for they, too, know that he is in charge.

Of Aslan, Narnians are fond of repeating, "He's not a tame lion." In *Battle*, Narnians use the statement to express sorrow and fear that perhaps the false Aslan is the real Aslan. Because he is not a tame lion, perhaps he indeed is having the talking trees cut down and the dwarfs and talking horses sold into slavery to the Calormenes. Many wonder if he is punishing them for some unknown fault.

To think that Aslan might do these things just because he isn't a tame lion means that Narnians have forgotten the second half of the truth: Aslan isn't safe and he isn't tame, but he is good. He obeys his own laws. He is bound by the Deep Magic in *Wardrobe*, even though it means his own death. He also became invisible in *Voyage* on the island where the Dufflepuds made living creatures magically invisible. If the citizens in the last days of Narnia had known and trusted his character, a pretender who looked a little bit like him from a distance but didn't act at all like him would not have deceived them.

King Tirian lends the others courage when he reminds them they are all between the paws of the true Aslan. Those paws are strong enough to destroy his enemies, but gentle enough to caress and protect his friends. This is very much like Jesus—the one who will judge the whole Earth, but whose gentleness was so great that children came to sit in His lap and grieving mothers came to Him to have their children restored to life. Indeed, we may love Aslan most for the ways he is most like Jesus.

Sometimes it is hard to know Jesus because we can't see Him or touch Him as the children could sometimes touch Aslan (with his permission). Yet the pages of the Bible show us story after story of His wisdom, His compassion, and His justice. We know enough about Him to be able to recognize someone who claims falsely to be coming in His name (as the Narnians should have done with the false Aslan in *Battle*)—because through Scripture, we know His character. Like Aslan, He does not lie, He does not change to become something different, and He keeps His promises.

He Died and Came to Life (for One Person)

In *Wardrobe*, one of the most moving scenes of the *Chronicles* woos us with its sorrowful love. The traitor Edmund deserves to die. Even though he is repentant, he cannot be restored to become one of the four kings and queens of Narnia, for a traitor's life is forfeit to the White Witch. Aslan offers the Witch an exchange she cannot refuse—his own life in trade for Edmund's. He willingly submits to death. He could give up on Edmund and start over again with someone more deserving, but he does not.

Even though he is dying for the disobedience of only one person, Aslan's death saves Narnia as a whole. For the prophecy cannot be fulfilled without four kings and queens, and that means Aslan needs Edmund. By fully restoring Edmund, Aslan is saving Narnia—and putting a humbled, strong leader on the throne.

Aslan goes to his death willingly but with great sadness. The scene may be very familiar because it is quite similar to that of Jesus in the Garden of Gethsemane before His crucifixion (Luke 22:42), praying to God the Father and saying He wished there was another way to save people from sin. But there wasn't another way. Our sin deserved death, and Jesus, being Himself perfect, was able to die in our place.

God Sightings

The word *sin* is never used in the *Chronicles*, but the concept is. Although most people will readily admit, "I'm not perfect," the word sin is a harder one for many people to use. That is because sin means wrong done against God. (Biblically, everything done against another person is also a sin against God.)

After Aslan was killed because of the Deep Magic, he came to life again because of the Deeper Magic (which the Witch didn't know about). Because he died as a willing victim and was innocent of the treachery he died for, death started working backward. That's a beautiful way to express what Jesus did. Because He was innocent of our sins and yet died for them, God the Father accepted His sacrifice as our own and raised Jesus from the dead.

He's the Creator (in a Limited Sense)

In *Nephew*, we see Aslan's role as creator of Narnia. Did he also create the land and waters that Aslan is about to bring to life? Did Aslan create the lands beyond Narnia, such as Archenland and Calormen, as well? We simply never find out. What we do know is that all the humans in Narnia are imported. All are sons of Adam and daughters of Eve, brought in from our world.

The Bible is clear that God began with absolutely *nothing* when He made the universe and populated this little planet. Everything we see around us is either something that God made or something that people or animals made from the materials He created.

He's Worthy of High Honor

Aslan can be trusted and obeyed, and he is good. It is safer to trust him than to disregard his instructions. As the Marsh-wiggle Puddleglum says in *Chair*, Aslan's instructions always work. Because he can be fully trusted, he must be fully obeyed, even when his subjects aren't sure of the outcome of obedience. What if they loose the bewitched knight who is swearing in the name of Aslan, and that wasn't really what Aslan meant for them to do? Jill and Eustace worry about that dilemma in *Chair*. But Puddleglum reasons that the results are not their problem.

They must obey and leave the results to Aslan. There are no accidents with Aslan, and surely he can be trusted even in this.

Sometimes Christians face the same dilemma. What the Bible tells us to do (or tells us not to do) is very difficult. Some other way seems more logical or safer, or even more pleasant. But because God is wiser than we are, and He knows a lot of things about us that we ourselves do not know, doing things His way works. And trusting Him is a good idea because He loves us and will take care of us.

Power in Aslan's Name

Aslan himself has great power, demonstrated in many areas, from his physical strength to his ability to foresee and even guide the future. (For instance, in *Horse*, we see much of his working behind the scenes to bring about the safety of Narnia and of the rightful heir to Archenland.)

But Aslan's name represents him, and thus even his name has mysterious power. In fact, on the day of creation, Aslan's creatures know his name without his having told them; they are his, and he is theirs.

Note the various feelings experienced by the children in *Wardrobe* when they first hear his name—before any of them has any idea who Aslan is. Edmund has a feeling of horror because he has already chosen the White Witch's side. The others have pleasant feelings in keeping with their own personalities. When the White Witch hears that Aslan is on the move, she is terrified—so much so that she soon warns her dwarf slave and Edmund that if either of them mentions Aslan's name again, he will be instantly killed.

When the green lady (really a witch) in *Chair* is thrumming her mandolinlike instrument and trying to put them under her spell to have them deny Narnia, Jill mentions Aslan. Aslan's name is enough to awaken Puddleglum to their danger. He stamps out the enchanted fire and insists that he will follow Aslan even if there isn't any Aslan. A fictional Aslan and a make-believe Narnia are better than a true witch and her underground world.

Characters swear by Aslan's name in various ways: "by Aslan," "by the Lion," or "by the Lion's mane," for instance. Bree's careless use of such terms means nothing; he really does not know who Aslan is. But others use similar terms as true acknowledgments of Aslan's authority. Prince Rilian shows Eustace, Jill, and Puddleglum his true identity by asking them to loose him in Aslan's name. Jill and Eustace call out to Aslan from England and find that he was calling to them as well and has prepared the way for them to enter his land.

Many parallels could be made between the uses of Aslan's name in the *Chronicles of Narnia* and Jesus' name in the Bible, as Lewis, of course, intended. Christians pray in the name of Jesus, use His name reverently, and hear His name as precious. Jesus' name causes Satan great anguish, as Aslan's name did the White Witch. Jesus' name even has a special meaning: "the one who saves."

Magic and Myth

Where did Aslan get his name? Lewis said he came across it in *One Thousand and One Nights*. Aslan is the Turkish word for "lion."

Coming in From Outside

Aslan is not a part of Narnia in a very real sense—he made it, so he is outside it. He does not live in Narnia. His presence is communicated from outside the world of Narnia. Yet because Aslan loves his creatures, he communicates with them in a way they can understand, and he loves them well.

Where Is He, Anyway?

Aslan doesn't appear often in Narnia, and when he does show up, sometimes it is for a very brief visit. Where is he between visits? The truest answer is that we don't really know. But these things we *do* know:

- He continues to watch over Narnia, whether or not he is physically present.
- Sometimes he is present but invisible.
- He is caring for other lands as well.
- Nothing happens in Narnia that he is powerless to control.

Aslan's Country

Aslan's country is a mystery until *Battle*, when Narnians who love Aslan are finally able to enter it—and stay. Until *Battle*, the main image of Aslan's country has been extraordinarily high mountains. In *Chair*, Jill and Eustace do not go directly into Narnia; instead, they enter through Aslan's country. From there, the trip to Narnia takes several hours of traveling on Aslan's breath, much of that being a trip *down* from the highest cliff imaginable. (When they return to England, they once again go through Aslan's country, although this time the trip is quicker.)

Before the end of Narnia, we know of two of Narnia's citizens who make it to Aslan's country. Reepicheep goes there by rowing to the utter east, and Caspian goes by dying of old age. The children see Caspian again in Aslan's country before they go back to England; Aslan brings him back to life there, and he is once again a young man. In *Voyage*, Caspian wants to abandon his shipmates and go straight on to Aslan's country as Reepicheep is doing, but it is only lawful for Reepicheep to do so. Caspian is the king and he has a responsibility to his country. Caspian has to wait—but he gets there at last.

By far the fullest picture of Aslan's country is in *Battle*, after Narnia ends. Those from our world who still love Aslan are there (through a train wreck), and we see again many from Narnia's earlier days, including King Frank and Queen Helen ... and Reepicheep.

Aslan's country, seen in *Battle*, encompasses all the best features of all lands. The children are delighted to see that it's Narnia, but better than Narnia ever was. But Aslan's country also has London and Tashbaan (from Calormen). And the children are only beginning to explore, so we can imagine Aslan's country has your city or town, too.

Puzzle, the donkey who was dressed to appear to be Aslan, shows up in Aslan's country as well. He was manipulated into his role in that deceit. Still, his role was wrong, and he is scared to meet Aslan. When the creatures have gone far enough into Aslan's country to be welcomed by Aslan, Puzzle is the first creature Aslan calls to him. After all, nobody made it into Aslan's country by good deeds. All are there because of their love for Aslan and, more important, his love for them—even Puzzle.

In one of the clearest indications that Aslan is Jesus, Aslan tells Edmund, Jill, and Eustace that there are doors to his country from our world as well. He tells them that the whole reason they came to Narnia in the first place is to know him better on Earth. In Aslan's country, the children are surprised to see Aslan looking less and less like a lion. The implication is not made directly, but it's clear—he is looking more and more like a man, the God-man Jesus.

Some Characters Changed by Aslan

Love him or hate him (and there are many characters in each camp), nobody is unaffected by Aslan. When he isn't present, plenty of people think it shows courage to speak of him disrespectfully. But when face to face with Aslan, even the White Witch picks up her skirts and runs for her life.

Many of Narnia's people choose evil and reject Aslan. But many others come face to face with him and are forever changed, in big or small ways. Let's look at several.

Lucy

Lucy is consistent in her love for Aslan and sees him on several occasions when the others do not (for instance, she knows he is the one who comes in the form of an albatross in *Voyage*, and she sees him at the gorge in *Caspian*). She trusts him and submits to him.

Lucy's love for others raises them higher. Tumnus is a good example. When he invites Lucy to his cave, it is with the purpose of kidnapping her. He finds he cannot do so and confesses his attempt. Lucy finds it hard to believe that such a "nice" faun would stoop to something so low. Once she believes him, she readily forgives him and considers him a dear friend from then on. He moves from the pay of the White Witch to the court of the true kings and queens, and we nearly forget he started out as an accomplice to a witch.

Lucy is easily one of the most pure-hearted characters in the series, even before she meets Aslan, and she immediately loves him. The lesson she most needs to learn is obedience.

In *Caspian*, Aslan gives Lucy a particularly hard test. Because of her great faith in him, she is the only one who sees him at the gorge and knows he expects her to follow. When the others refuse to believe her, she follows the group, though reluctantly. They learn later that they have made the wrong choice and wasted a lot of time, and Aslan chides Lucy for not following all by herself. Given a second chance (when, again, only Lucy sees Aslan), she says she will follow alone if she must. Only in such devotion is her love for him made complete.

Edmund

Edmund begins as a sneak, tiptoeing after his sister Lucy to spy on her; a liar, pretending never to have seen Narnia; an unkind brother, taunting Lucy even when they both know she is telling the truth; a glutton, willing to betray his family for Turkish Delight and a chance to be king someday; and, in general, a proud and selfish boy. Even when he knows he is wrong, he rationalizes his choices.

Two things change Edmund. First, he ends up as a slave of the White Witch long enough to know that he has made the wrong choice in following her. His pity for the innocent animals she has turned to stone is the beginning of his redemption. Second, Aslan forgives his treachery and instructs the others to do so as well. Edmund is humbled and truly changed.

Edmund never forgets his betrayal and never downplays or excuses it. In *Horse*, he wants Rabadash to have a chance to repent because "even a traitor may mend." After being forgiven his betrayal, Edmund never again wavers in his loyalty to Aslan or in his courage.

The White Witch's Statues

The power to raise the dead has never been presented more vividly as in the White Witch's courtyard of statues revived by Aslan (*Wardrobe*). God's breath first brought Adam to life, and Jesus' touch gave dead children back to their grieving parents. Thus, Aslan breathes on the statues, and they thaw from white marble into colorful, living, breathing beings. Not surprisingly, the newly awakened statues are eager to join in battle against the White Witch who imprisoned them in marble.

Here is where Edmund first shows his new courage. While Aslan is at the Witch's castle freeing the statues, the Witch is on the battlefront using her wand to make more statues. Instead of striking the Witch directly (and being made a statue himself in the attempt), Edmund swings his sword at her wand and breaks the wand, greatly limiting her power.

Eustace

Eustace rivals Edmund in "most odious character." He, too, is in urgent need of Aslan's redemption. In *Voyage*, we see numerous reasons that Eustace has gone wrong—and suspect Lewis hopes that parents might take note! Eustace is at a bad school, where he is bullied mercilessly; he is indulged by his mother; and he even reads the wrong books.

He is thoroughly selfish. On the ship, he complains incessantly and demands rights and privileges, looks for excuses to shirk work, argues with the crews' plans, and even attempts to steal water. When he is kidnapped and put up for auction as a slave, no one will buy him.

But then he meets Aslan. Before he does so, he has to get to the point of recognizing how needy he is. Eustace has seen himself as self-sufficient throughout the voyage—rather absurdly for one so powerless. He has rebuffed all efforts the others have made toward friendship, and he continues to put the worst possible spin on anyone's actions, assuming the worst motives of all those around him.

As a dragon, Eustace finds himself cut off from the others in a way that he didn't initiate. In his dragonish isolation, he becomes lonely. And for the first time in his life, he actually thinks about other people. (Although we suppose they aren't really "other people" to a dragon, now are they?) In a land of talking beasts, this dragon cannot talk, although he has all his human thoughts. For the first time, he is also beginning to have human feelings.

The formerly useless Eustace is able to help out in very meaningful ways: hunting large animals for his shipmates' food, spying out the island, and carrying back a full-size pine tree for a new mast for the ship. He realizes it matters to him that the others are beginning to like him.

And now Eustace is ready to meet Aslan.

Eustace is more than ready to be changed back into a boy. And he doesn't want to return to the boy he was; he himself shudders at that selfish wretch now. But he cannot change himself. Layer after layer of skin come off under his dragon claws, but he is still a dragon.

Eustace needs Aslan. He must submit to Aslan's claws, to the pain of having the skin ripped off whole, and then to being immersed naked in a pool, where he is healed. The stripping away of the old dragon, and even the skin of the old Eustace, is a wonderful picture of Christian conversion. We cannot make ourselves into the people we know we ought to be, or even the people we *want* to be. We must surrender and stop trying, and let Jesus take us and make us new. He can strip off the old, selfish, dragonish, self-centered person and cleanse and clothe us.

After Eustace's lesson, we are told that he began to be different. Soon he even does his first brave act, attempting to fight a sea serpent that is intent on destroying the ship. Of course, courage requires not thinking of one's own safety, but doing what needs to be done. Only now, freed of his obsession with himself, is he freed to be brave.

Bree and Hwin

The stallion Bree is like a young person who was the top of his class in a tiny junior high and expects to be top of his class in his large high school without studying. With the breeding of a Narnian talking horse and the training of a war horse, Bree thinks himself superior to everybody he meets.

If he is to do well in Narnia, he needs to recognize that in Narnia he will be an average talking horse, not the great horse he thought himself to be when he was among ordinary horses.

Even meeting Aslan doesn't change Bree much. He is speaking about Aslan, explaining foolishly that Aslan isn't really a lion, when Aslan himself shows up. Hwin goes to Aslan immediately, in joy and love, as Bree desires to flee. He sees that he has been wrong, but he still doesn't seek Aslan. His pride has been humbled a bit but not broken.

All through the journey, Bree has expressed a great desire to see Narnia. But the humble Hwin's desire for Narnia is purer. At the end, Bree is not in a hurry to enter because he is still too self-conscious. Instead of going into Narnia joyfully, he enters in gloom. Hwin is a free horse in Narnia; at least at the time he enters, Bree is still a slave because he is a slave to his pride.

Digory

In *Nephew*, the boy Digory has a high sense of honor, leading to indignation at his uncle's treatment of Polly. Yet Digory himself is selfishly impatient at Polly, interrupting her when she is hesitant about exploring other worlds from the Wood Between the Worlds. He grabs her wrist and pushes her with his body to keep her from getting to her ring when he wants to hit the bell in Charn and she (correctly) thinks it is unwise to do so.

Digory is unable to look Aslan straight in the eye at their first meeting because his conscience is guilty. But Aslan takes several steps to restore Digory by letting him undo the wrong he has done and protect Narnia. Digory is sent on a quest of great responsibility; Aslan gives him a lion kiss before he goes to lend him strength and courage. Aslan also empathizes over Digory's mother, crying over her illness and melting Digory's heart at his compassion.

When Digory returns with the apple that will protect Narnia by keeping the Witch away, Aslan allows Digory to plant it. Although Digory failed his first big test and awakened the Witch, Aslan's trust gives him confidence to pass his second test, the temptation to steal a second apple for his mother.

> **Magic and Myth**
>
> Charles Williams (1886–1945) was a friend of Lewis's and a member of the Inklings. His book *The Place of the Lion* featured an immense bright golden lion that appeared and disappeared at will and came with great mystery. Aslan is more clearly *good* than Williams's lion, but he is equally mysterious and awe inspiring.

Aslan compliments both the successful quest and the sowing, and Digory is enabled to look into his eyes. He is forgiven and restored.

Susan, Who Outgrows Her Belief

From the very beginning, Susan's inclination is to hold back and be absolutely sure of safety before she moves forward. She is inclined to trust Aslan as long as she can see him and see the results of trust. She is the one who is worried that a lion might not be safe and who wants to go back to England at every potential danger in *Wardrobe*. She continues to listen to her fears. She is the "practical" one of the group, unable to fully enter into the spirit of the adventure.

Lewis wrote about Susan (*Letters to Children*) that she was too grown-up, and once back in her own world she soon forgot about Narnia. He also points out that the series ends with Susan still alive in England, so she still has time to mend.

There are hints as early as *Caspian* that Susan is already forgetting Narnia. She looks at the king's dais and wonders aloud about the function of "that terrace kind of thing." Peter is shocked that she doesn't recognize it as a dais like the ones where they and their great lords sat. Susan seems like one in a dream as she says, of course, how could she forget their days in Cair Paravel?

Although Susan gains courage from her encounters with Aslan, she never has great faith. She can never get beyond her own safety. Are you more like Susan, the cautious one; or Lucy, the loving, self-forgetful, trusting one?

What Lewis Tells Us About Aslan

Lewis started *Wardrobe* with a picture of a faun, not a lion. Aslan came bounding into the story, but not initially as a picture of Jesus. Aslan just insisted on behaving his own way (as characters often do when authors write books—many authors say their characters surprise them by a statement or an action). When Aslan went willingly to his death, Lewis knew what he was really dealing with.

In many of Lewis's letters, undoubtedly in answer to repeated questions, he explains that Aslan is a "supposal" and not an allegory of Jesus. Aslan is his answer to the question, "Suppose there were another world in which people needed saving, and Jesus went into that world in a different physical form than He came into our world?"

The mother of one little boy wrote to Lewis for advice because her little boy was afraid he loved Aslan more than he loved Jesus. Lewis reassured her, telling her that probably the things he loved Aslan for were the things that are most like Jesus. In loving Aslan, he was really loving Jesus. He added that if it was the lion body that the little boy loved, then surely God would understand that, because he made little boys' imaginations.

There are many reasons to love Aslan and to be glad Lewis allowed him to come to life for us to know him.

The Least You Need to Know

- Aslan is rarely present in Narnia, showing up at times of great crisis and need, but generally leaving the land to the care of its human kings and queens.

- Aslan is a picture of Jesus Christ in several ways: his role as creator, his death and resurrection, his provision and care for his creatures, and his power.

- Relationship with Aslan changes people, if they submit to be loved by him and to obey him.

Chapter 6

Relationships in Narnia

In This Chapter

- Various relationships of people and other creatures in Narnia
- Family in Narnia
- C. S. Lewis's friendships, and how they affected his life and writing
- Aslan's relationships with others in Narnia

Narnia is a land of many peoples, from humans to giants, from talking horses to common mice and moles. To function as a society requires unity, relationship, and trust.

Friendship and comradeship form the backbone of many Narnian traditions. Friendship was the greatest joy of Lewis's life, and the *Chronicles* highlight relationships of all sorts: families, friendships, comrades in business or war, and teacher/student relationships.

Marriage and Family in Narnia

Most Narnian scenes take place in quests and community affairs such as dances or battles. We see very little of everyday family life. The family is still the basic unit of Narnian community, however, and we get a few looks at it.

Mr. and Mrs. Beaver

Mr. and Mrs. Beaver provide our best look at Narnian family life. Unfortunately, because they seem to be childless we see a marriage but no parenting. They appear to be a couple who has been married several years; they know each other well and love each other, but they have small habits that rub each other the wrong way or at least amuse each other. Mrs. Beaver fusses over everything, and she probably is late everywhere she goes. (At least, she is in no particular hurry to leave the house in spite of a very great threat that wolves and a witch may soon be headed to her home, so one can imagine that she feels no particular need to be on time for a lunch date.)

Mrs. Beaver plans ahead for every possibility—maybe a little too much, considering how much she loads everyone down when they're fleeing for their lives. Mr. Beaver is a good guide who takes the children safely to his home, to a cave that is used for beavers in hard times, and then on to the Stone Table. They seem to be a contented couple, in good relations with others around them and wanting to do the right thing for Narnia.

Fathers and Sons

We have several looks at fathers and sons in Narnia, particularly among its royalty, but they aren't detailed stories.

We don't see very much directly of the relationship between Caspian and his son Rilian. When *Chair* begins, Rilian has been missing for 10 years. Puddleglum, Jill, and Eustace rescue him from the Green Witch in time for his father to see him one last time—but just in time, as Caspian dies after welcoming his son home. We know, however, that Caspian has been in great grief at his loss, but he has forbidden people to continue to search for Rilian, having had many searchers die in the attempt.

Caspian's relationship with his own father was cut short by his father's early death, and he was raised by his uncle (Miraz) and aunt. When Caspian discovers that Miraz is a usurper who has taken Caspian's throne by treachery and murder, it means war. Not exactly an average family. (I'm not sure their photo albums would be worth looking at.)

Tirian, Narnia's last king, is overjoyed to be reunited with his father in the new Narnia and kisses him in welcome. We see little of their reunion but we learn that seeing his father brings back the smell of bread-and-milk suppers, a cozy memory. Apparently they had a loving relationship.

King Lune of Archenland is a wise, loving father to his son Corin in *Horse*, and later to Corin's twin brother, Cor. He takes the responsibility of a king seriously and trains his sons to be wise and loving leaders. Glenstorm the centaur comes to meet Caspian, along with his three sons, when Caspian is gathering Old Narnians to his side. Glenstorm speaks boldly of their readiness for war.

In summary, we see enough glimpses to know that fathers and sons are important to one another in Narnia, but not enough to know much about their relationships. Lewis probably didn't know how to say a whole lot more than he did, never having had a son, having a strained relationship with his father, and growing up in an era when men really didn't talk about family relationships all that much.

Lewis did finally get a bit of a taste of parenting shortly after the *Chronicles* were published. When he married Joy Davidman, he became a stepfather to her two sons, David and Douglas, and he continued to raise them after her death. He grew especially fond of Douglas, although David was at an age when family losses were especially difficult, and David and Lewis never grew very close.

Other Families

We know more about Prince Caspian's family than that of any other character in the *Chronicles*. We know bits and pieces of his family tree, from the first Caspian, known as Caspian the Conqueror, a Telmarine who took over Narnia; to the last king of Narnia, Tirian, who says that he is the seventh in descent from Rilian (Caspian's son). But this is hardly a functional family when we first meet them—Caspian's own father, Caspian IX, was murdered by his brother (Caspian X's uncle), Miraz, who then ruled for many years.

Ramandu and his daughter are another family we meet in *Voyage*, though no wife and mother is mentioned. Ramandu and his daughter take care of World's End Island and watch over Aslan's table, which has luxurious foods provided daily for any visitors and the birds from the sun. We know little of their relationship except that it seems a respectful, affectionate one.

Quite a few groups of housemates in Narnia are apparently bachelors, and most likely brothers. The Bulgy Bears of *Caspian* fit in this category, although we don't know for sure whether this trio of brown bears is all male or what their relationship is. The Seven Brothers of Shuddering Wood are dwarfs who work together in a smithy.

One brief glimpse of an entire family—mother, father, and children— is all we are given in *Wardrobe*. A family of squirrels, along with friends, is feasting on food provided by Father Christmas. One baby squirrel gets nervous and chatters when it should be silent, and the White Witch turns the whole party to stone in her wrath. We know nothing more of them.

We do see at least one other married couple in Narnia besides the beavers: the giant king and queen of Harfang. Jill, Eustace, and Puddleglum have gone to Harfang to be part of the giants' autumn feast. (Without going into the details, let's just say that had they known what part they were expected to play in the festivities, they would have written a polite "no thanks" to RSVP for the invitation.) Anyway, the giants gladly welcome them and offer them great food and comfortable sleeping quarters. We first see the king and queen dressed splendidly on side-by-side thrones, and the next day we see the queen on a litter, being carried by courtiers, as the king and 20 or 30 other giants are ready to set out on a hunt.

Missing Parents

Oddly, nowhere in the *Chronicles* do we see a mother and father and their children (except for that unfortunate squirrel family)—neither in Narnia nor in England. The closest we come is the early years in Rilian's family, before the story begins and before the green serpent killed his mother.

The Pevensie children are sent out of London because of the war, and they are staying with the Professor in his home. From there they go through the wardrobe to Narnia. They have parents, but they never come into the story. Their cousin, Eustace Scrubb, has parents as well, although very modern parents whom he calls by their first names, and we don't see them directly either.

Caspian is an orphan, and Rilian is motherless. Shasta in *Horse* is living with a man he believes to be his father but who actually is not; when this father figure is willing to sell him into slavery, it propels him into running away. Digory Kirke (*Nephew*) is staying at his uncle's house while his father is away in India and his mother is dying.

So both in England and in Narnia, we have mostly children with only one parent or none—a fact that might help readers who are children of single parents find a connection, especially if they are mourning the loss of one of their own parents.

Where Are All the Women?

Most of the characters we meet in Narnia are male. In fact, several entire species show no female representative in the books, including dwarfs, centaurs, and fauns. (We do see several giantesses in Harfang.) Most of the talking animals are male as well. But part of the "maleness" is really generic; unless there is a reason for an animal to be female (say, as part of a couple), the animal is male.

The children who come into Narnia from London are balanced equally between boys and girls: the Pevensies have two boys (Peter and Edmund) and two girls (Susan and Lucy). The first time Eustace Scrubb comes, it is with Edmund and Lucy, making an odd number of visitors, but the second time he comes with Jill Pole. At the very beginning of Narnia, Digory Kirke and Polly Plummer come together; they also bring other people (and a horse), but the children themselves are one boy and one girl.

Friendships in Narnia

In Narnia, friendships are very important. We see several different kinds of friendship. Let's look at three: one between two men (same gender, same species), one between a man and a unicorn (same gender, different species), and one between a lion and a girl (different gender, different species). All of these friendships are between a greater and a lesser authority, but all are true, intimate friendships nonetheless.

Lewis dealt in several books with what he called "inner-ring" friendships (most notably in *That Hideous Strength*). These are attempts to seek power by befriending those who have social or political power. They are not really friendships as much as they are a form of gang mentality, using people as a means to an end. So it's notable that some of the closest friendships in the *Chronicles* are between a sovereign and a subject—but they are friendships of equals in spite of the power difference.

Lewis says that no pleasure compares to Christian friends sitting together by a good fire, and he calls friendship the greatest joy of his life. His companionship included lengthy hikes, chats by the fire, and Inklings meetings (see Chapter 1) to discuss literature. The simple companionship of these friendships shows up in Narnia.

Lord Drinian and King Caspian

Lord Drinian is captain of the *Dawn Treader* in *Voyage*. Thus, he and King Caspian each have respect for the other and submit to the other's expertise. The king can make decisions that override the captain, but on issues of navigation, he generally accepts the greater knowledge of the captain. The men lend strength to each other's decision making. King Caspian has authority, but Lord Drinian has wisdom and age. Lewis's longest job, as an Oxford don, prepared him to write convincingly about mentoring relationships between older and younger men. The boy Caspian and his tutor are another example of a close, yet uneven relationship in terms of age and rank.

In *Chair*, Caspian is married with a young adult son, Rilian. Drinian is concerned about a young woman who is drawing Rilian to meet her every day, but he waits too late to speak to the king of his concern, and Rilian disappears. Drinian's failure to speak is a grave error, and Caspian almost executes Drinian for it. But he realizes that he must not lose his son and his friend in the same day, and he forgives him.

Magic and Myth

When Lewis's friend Charles Williams died suddenly, his death affected Lewis deeply. In *The Four Loves*, Lewis remarked that once Williams was gone, Lewis had less not only of Williams, but also of their mutual friend Tolkien. He meant that each friend brings out a different part of a person, and the addition of friends adds depth to one's own life and the lives of all they touch.

King Tirian and Jewel

When we first meet King Tirian in *Battle*, he is in his early twenties but already an experienced warrior. His dearest friend is Jewel the unicorn, with whom he was in the battles. Each of them had saved the other's life, and they loved each other like brothers.

One might think that a friendship between a man and a unicorn would not be a relationship of equals, especially if that man is a king. But a unicorn is no ordinary beast, or even an ordinary talking horse, and theirs is a friendship of many years. They are able to advise each other, protect each other, and comfort each other in the dark days that enter Narnia in the course of the book. As they prepare to go into their final battle together, they ensure that neither friend has anything unforgiven against the other. They enter their final battle sad but resolute.

Navigating Narnia

Lewis frequently said his favorite sound was adult male laughter. He liked nothing better than companionship with like-minded people—and that meant people who liked books.

Aslan and Lucy

One doesn't immediately think of "friendship" between Aslan and Lucy, but we think the word fits. Clearly, they love each other, and each draws strength from the other. (When Aslan was about to submit to being killed by the White Witch, he asked Lucy and Susan to lay their hands on his mane so that he could feel their presence and be strengthened by it.)

Lucy can sometimes be faulted for slow obedience, but never for lack of love. She sees Aslan on several occasions when others do not. On one of these times, in *Caspian*, the Pevensies and Trumpkin the dwarf are together at the gorge, deciding which way to go to get to Aslan's How. Lucy sees Aslan and knows that he is telling them to follow him. The others don't see him, and they vote to go a different way.

Lucy is torn but goes with her traveling companions, crying bitterly. She is not yet strong enough to choose Aslan over such peer pressure, though later Aslan tells her she should have followed alone. When they return from their failed attempt, Aslan appears again, and again Lucy is the only one to see him. The discussion leads to annoyance on all sides, but Lucy looks at Aslan and forgets her own annoyance—his face is more important than anything else. Now she is willing to follow, even if she must follow alone. She is willing to put Aslan above her family and friends if he asks that of her.

God Sightings

Jesus calls Himself a friend of His followers (Luke 12:4). In Christianity, it's possible for a person to be a friend of God. Moses is given the incredibly high honor of speaking face to face with God, as to a friend (Exodus 33:11). Abraham is called God's friend (Isaiah 41:8; James 2:23). And we ourselves can be Jesus' friends (John 15:13–15).

When Aslan tells her at the end of the voyage that she cannot return to Narnia, she is very sad. In *Battle*, when she is in Aslan's country, the new Narnia, King Tirian looks at Lucy and sees that she is too happy to speak. Being with Aslan is all she wants. In his presence, she is content. She and Reepicheep, who wants nothing more than Aslan's country, are different but complementary pictures of the Christian life—both want to be with Jesus more than anything else.

Other Relationships in Narnia

Besides Narnian families and friends, we see some other associations. Although we rarely see Narnians work, we do see battle scenes and schooling situations.

Comrades and Fellow Soldiers

In Narnia, battle is a serious thing. Major battles determine who will rule Narnia (the White Witch or the Pevensies, Caspian or his uncle Miraz) or whether Calormen will destroy Narnia, as it would love to do. Narnians must fight well, fight hard, and fight together. Each warrior fights as he fights best.

Those who battle together develop respect for others' strengths and learn to support each other's vulnerabilities. Reepicheep the mouse cannot fight chest to chest with grown men and large animals—but he can stab ankles and thus distract or even trip an enemy. No one who has fought alongside Reepicheep laughs at him. He comes out of the battle for Caspian's kingship heavily wounded; Lucy's cordial and Aslan's healing are both necessary to restore him. His mice are willing to cut off their own tails for him because of his loyalty to them.

In *Voyage*, the governor of the Lone Islands is no longer interested in allegiance to the king of Narnia (who is also the emperor of the Lone Islands). The *Dawn Treader* doesn't have enough warriors to retake the islands in battle, so King Caspian, Lord Drinian, and Lord Bern work together to appear to have battleships ready to retake the islands. Thus, they avoid a battle they would be unable to win.

Teachers and Students

We see only one good teacher/student relationship in Narnia: that of the boy Caspian and his tutor, Dr. Cornelius. Dr. Cornelius is wise about how to teach Caspian, knowing far more than he tells, and knowing when and how to tell Caspian what the prince needs to know. He teaches him history, politics, grammar, and all the other necessary lessons for a young prince. But late at night, he also teaches him the forbidden, true history of Old Narnia and of his family heritage. When it becomes necessary, he sends Caspian to flee for his life, offering help and wisdom, and meeting up with him again later.

Other mentions of schooling in the *Chronicles* are almost universally negative, whether the school is in England or Narnia. Eustace and Jill go to a very bad school, Experiment House. It was at a "horrid" school that Edmund began to go wrong, bullying smaller children.

On the list of ways that the Pevensies ruled wisely and well was the fact that they "liberated young dwarfs and young satyrs from being sent to school" *(Wardrobe)*. At the end of *Caspian*, Aslan releases the students at a girls' school and turns the swinish students at a boys' school into little pigs so that their teacher can be freed from trying to teach them.

Parents reading this book aloud to their children have told us of their distress at the repeated anti-school comments; perhaps Lewis would have done better to leave some of them out. But surely the comments help some children know that he identified with the joys and sorrows of childhood, even the times that attending school is a burden.

When the Pevensies are slow to realize that they can stay in Aslan's country, the new Narnia, forever and never have to go back to London, Aslan explains by telling them "The term is over: the holidays have begun" *(Battle)*.

The Least You Need to Know

- In Narnia, relationships are the primary cultural and social force.
- We see very little of family life in Narnia or among its child visitors.
- Aslan is a very personal king, developing deep relationships with many of his subjects.

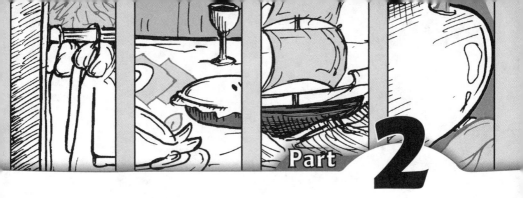

Part 2

Book by Book: Into the World of Narnia

We've had a chance to look at the background of *The Chronicles of Narnia*. Now let's look at the books themselves: the major characters, themes, and background influences of each book in the series. Aslan shows up in all the books, and the Pevensie children show up in most of them. We'll get to know King Caspian and some odd Narnian creatures. We will explore Narnia from its remotest North to its untraveled Eastern Sea. If you're packed and ready, let's go.

Chapter 7

The Lion, the Witch and the Wardrobe

In This Chapter

- The first book published in the *Chronicles of Narnia*
- A first look at many elements of Narnian life: its creatures, warfare, interaction with Earth, and Aslan
- The White Witch's power over Narnia and her defeat at the paws of Aslan
- The Pevensie children's first visit(s) to Narnia

What child could help falling in love with Aslan, a talking lion who rules over a land of talking beasts—and who calls children from our world to be its kings and queens or to rescue Narnia in time of trouble?

Narnia is a land with frightening evils, including fearsome giants and talking wolves, and a witch who can freeze her enemies to stone with a flick of her wand. The land itself has had 100 years of winter under the White Witch's wicked reign. But with Aslan's great sacrifice and the entry of four prophesied human children, the Witch's power—and her life—are about to end.

Narnia has a combination of cozy, everyday life (good friends and tasty food) and the fantastic (talking trees, dancing fauns, magical white stags). It feels enough like home to want to stay, but different enough for us to long to go back. Most important, Aslan is there.

Fast Facts

Wardrobe was published in 1950. This book has important lessons on integrity, forgiveness, and sacrifice—but first the Pevensie children must brave an enchanted winter and find Aslan before it's too late.

Navigating Narnia

What does it mean when the Pevensie children are called sons of Adam and daughters of Eve? The children are human descendants of Adam and Eve, the first people. Read about them in the first few chapters of the Bible's first book, Genesis. But be warned—some of the story isn't very nice.

According to Lewis's Outline of Narnian History, the Pevensies ruled from 1000 to 1015 Narnian time. Lucy entered the wardrobe first, followed by a second brief visit by Lucy and Edmund. A third visit brought all four children—who then grew up in Narnia as its rulers but returned to England in the same hour Earth time that they left, as young boys and girls all over again.

Much is frozen in Narnia when the story starts: the country is frozen in winter, Edmund has a frozen heart, and the Witch has a courtyard of statues (animals and other creatures that she has frozen). Aslan comes to thaw and to rescue.

Who Will We Meet?

Because this book was the first one published, we have a full introduction to many characters, to the types of beings who populate Narnia, and to Narnia itself. Let's meet the most significant ones.

The Pevensie Children: Peter, Susan, Edmund, Lucy

Lewis wrote in a letter to his brother about modern children who can't entertain themselves. In the *Chronicles*, the children not only entertain themselves in a large, unfamiliar house, but they know what to do in the strange country of Narnia (such as following the robin). That's largely because of reading the right books—unlike Eustace in *Voyage*.

Of course, modern children usually don't have to be independent at an early age like Lewis did—entertaining himself while his widowed father was at work and then attending boarding school.

From the Narnian perspective, human children are the mythical beings in this story. Both Tumnus the faun and the White Witch are shocked by humans' appearance in Narnia—although the Beavers and Aslan are expecting them.

> **Navigating Narnia**
>
> In *Wardrobe*, the robin at the story's beginning and the mice who nibble Aslan's ropes after his death understood but did not speak—the only time in the series we have such animals. They can probably be equated with a pet who has a good relationship with its owner and understands the owner's desires.

We first meet the children in England, in a big old house in the country where they have been sent to get away from the air raids of London during World War II. Interestingly, the Pevensies' last name is never mentioned in this book, but we learn it in *Caspian*. Let's meet the Pevensie children from youngest to oldest, because that is the order in which they entered Narnia.

Gentle Lucy

Lucy is the gentle, loving one, with a deep love for Aslan. In *Wardrobe*, she loans her handkerchief twice, showing her generosity: to a faun who meant to kidnap her and to a giant. One of her few negative choices in the series comes late in this book, when her desire to see Edmund's healing causes her to procrastinate about obeying Aslan's command to go and heal others.

Lucy is very truthful—her siblings don't believe her when she tells them about Narnia, but she can't tell them she made up Narnia because she didn't. Her siblings' unbelief causes a rift between them, which deeply distresses the sensitive, gentle Lucy. What draws Lucy into the wardrobe is her love for the feel of fur. Later, she loves to caress Aslan's living fur.

Navigating Narnia

Wardrobe has by far the most detailed dedication from the series, to Lucy Barfield, Lewis's goddaughter. Lucy was 12 when Lewis began writing, nearly 15 when *Wardrobe* was released. The dedication tells her that books grow faster than girls, but she will someday be old enough again to read the book. Lucy Pevensie is probably named for this Lucy.

The Betrayer, Edmund

Edmund starts out as a villain, a boy gone badly wrong. Turkish Delight is his initial temptation, but his real temptation is to dominate, to gain power over younger kids at school and Peter. Edmund's wrong-doing is portrayed realistically, as a gradual descent into evil.

His wrong choices are numerous: he is spiteful, proud, bullying, and lying, and ultimately he chooses to betray his own family and Aslan. He rationalizes his sin, nursing hatred of Peter. He is easily tempted by the Witch's flattery: this greedy, sticky-faced boy became, in her words, the cleverest and handsomest boy she knew, worthy of being a prince.

He is willing to keep his meeting with the Witch a secret at her request, knowing that secrecy improves his chances of betraying the others.

He is actually risking the loss of his only genuine chance to be king. According to the prophecy, he is supposed to be a king of Narnia, but with the responsibilities kingship entails and not just endless privilege. To him, being king means getting rich and getting what one desires. He needs to learn concern for others before he is actually ready to rule.

On Edmund's return to Narnia, with all four children, the destruction of Tumnus's cave and the note signed in the Witch's name should be enough to warn Edmund away from further interaction with her—but he is bewitched and longs to fulfill his own desires. (Edmund asks Peter how he knows it is a nice beaver they're following—an oddly scrupulous question from someone who'd willingly follow a known witch!)

Deep down inside, he knows the white lady is really a witch. He somehow expects her to treat him kindly anyway but is quickly disillusioned. First, he hears that the danger to his siblings is real: the wolf is given permission to *kill* his brother and sisters and the beavers. But even he himself no longer seems such a favorite: he requests Turkish Delight but gets stale bread and water. And then begins the long, cold journey when he begins to repent.

Edmund is not fully invested in evil; he simply is self-centered and wants his own desires met. But his self-centeredness allows him to tolerate other evils, and putting himself first is a greater evil than he can see. Later, finally, we are told he is not thinking of himself anymore (he is too interested in looking at Aslan), and then, as a king, he is known as Edmund the Just.

After the battle, when Edmund is restored with Lucy's cordial, he is back to his old self "before he began to go wrong" at school—he has fought bravely and made up for his wrong. He can now look others in the face again. But his restoration isn't easy: it takes Aslan's death and his own serious injury. Lewis believed that schools often brought out the worst in young pupils, because children are seeking their own place. Inevitably, some children seek popularity even at the cost of cruelty to others, and Edmund had fallen into that trap before he was rescued by an up-close look at pure evil and self-seeking in the form of the Witch.

The Older Ones, Susan and Peter

From the very beginning of the adventures, Susan seeks safety first. She doesn't want to stay in Narnia if it means uncertainty about where the next meal will come from, or the danger of meeting up with the ones who destroyed Tumnus's home. She is concerned whether Aslan is safe and whether it will be safe for Aslan to restore a giant who has been turned into stone. (Note to Susan: no, lions and giants and witches aren't safe. That's the whole point.) Ironically, at the end, she's the one who's reluctant to follow the white stag that actually proves to be the end of their adventures, because following him returns them back through the wardrobe and into England.

Susan is bossy, trying to be a grown-up. We see different parts of the story through the eyes of different children, and Susan is the one who takes leadership in the scene of Aslan's death.

As the firstborn, Peter will be the high king over all kings—which lends him responsibility far beyond the few years of his active reign. Before Aslan's death, Aslan gives Peter the battle strategy but leaves him to command the army, a mighty responsibility for a teenage boy in a new land. He doesn't feel brave when Susan blows her horn and he is sent to defend her, but he kills the wolf before it can kill her. By nature, Peter isn't a risk-taker, but he is an explorer and is willing to step forward and take responsibility that is his duty.

Knowing and doing one's duty is a big part of Lewis's focus. He believed that to do otherwise is neither moral nor a good route to happiness. In his own life, he dutifully cared for a household, tutored students, and answered endless letters from his readers, on days he wanted to and days he didn't.

The Professor

The Professor is host to the Pevensie children, although there is no indication he knows them or their family personally before the story begins. He is described as a very old man with shaggy white hair over most of his face. In his large, rambling country house, the adventures begin as the children enter a wardrobe in a spare bedroom.

Magic and Myth

In the short story *The Aunt and Amabel* by E. Nesbit, a bored little girl in her aunt's spare room finds an unusual station in a train schedule: Bigwardrobeinspareroom, traveling to Whereyouwanttogoto. She opens the wardrobe door and goes for a trip. Lewis had read the story as a boy but apparently had forgotten it, although it could have influenced *Wardrobe*.

When Peter and Susan come to him with their concerns about Lucy and her made-up country, he listens carefully without interrupting. Then he asks, "How do you know that your sister's story is not true?" He takes truth very seriously, as does Lucy herself; he tells them that a charge of lying is a very serious one if the person is known to be truthful.

The Professor uses the Socratic Method (drawing a learner to knowledge by asking questions) with the children, asking eight questions in three pages, and replying to their questions not with answers, but with further questions.

The Professor seeks to instill logic in the children. That something is unexpected doesn't mean it's untrue; Peter and Susan are starting with the assumption that their sister's tale is not true, and he undercuts that assumption. (In *Nephew*, we find that the Professor was once a little boy named Digory Kirke, and he himself has been to Narnia.)

God Sightings

In *Mere Christianity*, Lewis says that Jesus made clear assertions that He was God. A man making such claims could truly be God, could be a liar, or could be insane—but he could not be merely "a great moral teacher," as some call Jesus without accepting His claim to be God. The Professor gives these same three choices for Lucy—she is lying, she is telling the truth, or she is insane.

A Faun, Mr. Tumnus

Tumnus seems friendly and hospitable at our first meeting. He invites Lucy home for tea and rather insists on her joining him. He takes Lucy home to a cozy cave with a fire, a kettle, and a good English tea.

Alas, he has less than hospitable motives; he fully intends to turn this young human over to the White Witch. He finds he cannot do so and admits his plan to Lucy.

Tumnus is familiar with mythology, as a look at his bookcase will soon prove. *Is Man a Myth?* sits among other similar titles there. He recognizes Lucy's identity fairly quickly. He also remembers the Narnian prophecy about humans sitting on the four thrones of Cair Paravel. While human beings remained "mythical" to him, he could imagine turning them over to the Witch, but getting to know a real person makes his treachery impossible.

Lucy's forgiveness is heartfelt: she willingly trots off to visit him each time she ends up in Narnia and insists that she and her family must rescue him from the White Witch's clutches. She looks for him in the White Witch's hall of statues, and they are happily reunited. This unlikely friendship takes Tumnus from the pay of the White Witch to honor in the court of the Pevensies.

The White Witch

The White Witch is clothed in white fur, with a golden wand and crown, a pale face, and a red mouth. She's beautiful, but proud, cold, and stern—especially cold. If we could use only one word to describe a witch who'd brought 100 years of winter, *cold* would be it.

The Witch is distressed to find that the doors from the world of men really do exist and that Edmund is a hint of the prophecy of her own destruction. She raises her wand—first-time readers of the book may not recognize the significance of that action, and Edmund does not. But plenty of statues in her courtyard testify to the power of that wand and what she was about to do to Edmund. (Edmund later discovers that her power is greatly diminished without her wand.) The statues in her courtyard are similar to the "waxworks" in *Nephew*—the people she froze in time in her original land, Charn.

The White Witch claims for herself the high titles of a legitimate ruler of Narnia, which, of course, she is not. She cannot make eye contact with Aslan; her only power is with the claims of the Deep Magic. When Aslan voluntarily surrenders himself instead of Edmund, she believes she has won—as Satan perhaps believed when Jesus was killed on the cross—but Aslan's death is her undoing. He comes back to life and destroys her. At long last, Narnia is fully out from under her power.

When she came to the Stone Table to speak to Aslan, everyone felt cold. Her wintry power may be limited, but she still retains some power. The Stone Table on which she kills Aslan is a great grim slab of stone, resting on four upright stones. Even the knife used to kill Aslan is made of stone, and her enemies are turned to stone. Her whole power is of death, not life.

Magic and Myth

These days, a white witch often means a practitioner of "white magic," a good witch. Lewis didn't have to contend with the cultural idea of a "good witch" (like Glinda in *The Wizard of Oz* and some of the girl students in the Harry Potter books). To him, a white witch was a recognizable archetype, a cold, frozen witch.

The Stone Table's being broken in two after Aslan came alive again is much like the veil in the temple being torn after Jesus died (Matthew 27:51). The veil was very thick, and it represented separation between God and man. God was too holy to let sinful people come close to Him. But Jesus' death made a way for people to go to God safely, with Jesus' sacrifice paying for their sins. The thick veil was no longer needed. Here in Narnia, the Deeper Magic destroyed the Deep Magic and broke the Stone Table.

Mr. and Mrs. Beaver

The children enter Narnia tentatively, not sure where to go or what they should do. But that has already been decided for them. Their first order of business is given by Mr. Beaver, who tells them "further in, come further in." This will be echoed in the new Narnia, as the refrain is repeated numerous times in *Battle*.

Mrs. Beaver prepares for the trip to the Stone Table—mothering the children and making sure they all have what they need to eat and sleep on the journey. She is calmer than the others. She is not being careless with safety (although the more nervous members of the crew think she is), but careful for proper provision.

God Sightings

Mr. Beaver told the children that the White Witch was descended from Adam's first wife, Lilith. Lilith comes from other Jewish mythology, not from the Bible, and in some understandings she is a female demon. Biblically Adam's only wife was Eve, who was made from his side by God.

When spring comes, the beavers and children are dreamy and quiet inside. Traveling by foot as the woods change from winter to spring, they have a good view of the change and rejoice in it, for it speaks of Aslan's nearness. Under the Witch, they have suffered endless winter and dangers from her rule; Aslan is righting the land, starting with the seasons. This could possibly be equated to God's assertion, after the major catastrophe of the Flood in Genesis, that for the rest of Earth's history spring and summer would follow winter, without fail (Genesis 8:22), showing His loving control over everything.

Father Christmas

One of the first things Lucy learned about the Witch was that in her many years of winter, she had kept Christmas out. Clearly, Father Christmas's presence is a sign of her power crumbling, and he gives gifts that are important to the story line. He's not funny and jolly, like Santa Claus, but big and glad, solemn and joyful (a common combination for good characters in the *Chronicles*). Father Christmas is the British Santa Claus, in case you're wondering. That thing about Santa visiting the whole world in one night ... well, never mind.

Narnian Dictionary

The **incarnation** took place when Jesus came to Earth and became human. His life didn't start then, but His humanity did. He didn't stop being God; the incarnation means Jesus is now both God and man. He had to become human to die for our sins, so at Christmas time we celebrate His birth, but we are also celebrating His death and resurrection for us.

Tolkien, Roger Lancelyn Green, and others recommended against Lewis's use of Father Christmas. Christmas really doesn't seem to fit into a world without the *incarnation*. But his presence in the story was important to Lewis, and important for the story in its own way.

The presents for the children are important ones. Peter receives a shield and a sword (with the lion on them); Susan, a bow and arrows and an ivory horn that summons help, even from across worlds; Lucy, a dagger and a diamond bottle full of a healing cordial (juice of fire-flowers from the mountains of the sun). Father Christmas is not bringing toys for their amusement; he is preparing them in advance for the battle they must soon enter. He is like the Holy Spirit, equipping the Christian believer ahead of time with what will be needed (Ephesians 6:10-17).

Aslan

Aslan is both good and terrible—never more than in this book, where we see his wrath against the Witch and his mercy toward Edmund. He deposes and executes the White Witch and reestablishes rightful rule in Narnia. We also see the cost at which he dealt with Edmund's treachery—his own life.

After surrendering himself to the Witch, Aslan walks openly to his enemies, making no resistance, even when they spitefully shave and mock him. And then the Witch kills him. This whole scene is very similar to the crucifixion of Jesus, recorded in all four Gospels (the first four books of the New Testament). Read about it in John 19.

After the brutal forces leave, Susan and Lucy come out of hiding and approach the body. Like the women at Christ's tomb caring for His body, the girls unmuzzle Aslan and try to untie him, but the mice must do that. The girls cry till they have no tears left and walk away, physically and emotionally spent.

Soon they hear a deafening noise, a sound described as being as if a giant had broken a giant's plate. It is the Stone Table, cracked in two. Aslan is alive and larger than ever. As he will later do with Shasta in *Horse*, he licks Susan's forehead to prove he's alive and not a ghost. After Jesus' death and resurrection, He ate food to show He wasn't a ghost, and suggested that His doubting disciple, Thomas, should feel His wounds to see it was really Him, in a real body.

So how can Aslan come back to life? The Deeper Magic. As a willing victim who committed no treachery, dying in a traitor's stead, his death defeats the power of death. We are told in Scripture that Jesus returned to life because God accepted His sacrifice for our sins.

> ### God Sightings
>
> We know little about Aslan's father, the Emperor-Beyond-the-Sea, but it is his scepter that put the Deep Magic into Narnia. He is the equivalent of God the Father in the Christian Trinity (one God in three persons). The Chronicles don't have an equivalent to the Holy Spirit, but it has been noted that Father Christmas gives gifts, fulfilling one of the Holy Spirit's functions.

Over and over in the *Chronicles*, we are told that Aslan isn't a tame lion. Yet one of the first things he does after his resurrection is play with children. In a further twist of normal expectations, Aslan leaps over the sacred Stone Table, and Lucy scrambles over it to reach him. After the romp, he roars with a terrible face and then takes the girls on his back to the Witch's castle to rescue her statuesque victims.

Aslan's death is unexpected and sad, but his resurrection is unexpected and joyful—what Tolkien called a eucatastrophe, or a joyful turn of events when you expect only gloom.

Other People

Wardrobe presents a vast range of characters. The Pevensies are the only humans in Narnia in this book, but in addition to the characters we have already mentioned, we see mythical characters, including tree girls (dryads, further developed in later books, particularly *Caspian*); the good giant Rumblebuffin, awakened by Aslan and loaned Lucy's handkerchief; merpeople singing at the children's coronation; and many other creatures.

> ### Navigating Narnia
>
> Where did Lewis get the name for Narnia? Possibly from the mountain village of Narnia, now called Narni, in the Italian province of Umbria.

We see talking animals from a vast multitude of species, mostly on Aslan's side, but many on the Witch's. Her crew includes numerous evil species: animals gone bad, ghouls and ogres, boggles, minotaurs, cruels, hags, specters, and many more.

And then at the end, it's a white stag that takes the children back to England. We don't hear how Narnians reacted when their kings and queens left to chase a stag and never returned. But the Pevensies themselves made it into the Narnian history books as rulers during Narnia's Golden Age, so apparently there were no hard feelings.

What Should We Watch For?

Wardrobe is packed so full that entire books have been written on just this one book, so we have a lot to look for as we read it. Lewis said much about people, about life, and about God. Let's look at some of the most important things we might miss.

How Can One's Own Failings Blind and Trap Him?

The White Witch easily deceives Edmund because he is driven by his personal desires. He is wooed first by magic candy and then by the greater desire to lord it over his older brother by being king.

Navigating Narnia

Just what *is* Turkish Delight? It's a rectangular fruit-flavored jelly candy rolled in a coating, often of powdered sugar. Few people like it as much as Edmund does. Think of extra-chewy Jell-O rolled in sugar, and you'll be close. It's hard to find in the United States but is readily available in Europe.

How Does Evil Appear Good?

To a discerning child, the Witch would not appear to be a friend. But Edmund has already begun to choose evil, and the Witch is sly. She knows how to appeal to his appetites and rope him in. He is suspicious of her at first. She starts giving him what he wants (not what he needs) and flattering him. Then she offers to help him with what he wants most—a way to outdo Peter. His defenses are overridden, and he convinces himself that she is really good, or at least that she will be good *to him*. (Alas, that is all he cares about.)

How Does Good Win over Evil?

After a hundred years of winter (and never Christmas), the White Witch's magic has a solid grip on Narnia. Her evil folk are numerous. She wins by power and fear. But Aslan is more powerful. At his coming, he begins to undo her magic. The children's arrival in Narnia is the first hint that her power is coming to an end. Aslan's thaw and the presence of Father Christmas indicate that it is unraveling quickly. The power of the Deeper Magic, unveiled in Aslan's sacrifice, proves to be her final undoing, awaiting only her execution to finish the job.

Lewis believed that evil was only a twisting of good. In *Mere Christianity* he wrote that badness is "spoiled goodness," even a "parasite" on what is good, and therefore of lesser power. The Witch's power lasts only until Aslan shows up and defeats her.

Forgiveness also holds great power: Lucy's forgiveness of Tumnus and then everyone's forgiveness of Edmund.

The power of good doesn't always come in big ways. When Lucy and Susan cannot remove the rope from the dead Aslan, mice nibble through it—and in *Caspian*, we discover that Aslan made them talking mice in gratitude for that loving deed.

As Aslan breathes on the statues, the deadly white turns into a blaze of colors, noisy with animal sounds, shouts, and songs and laughter. The scene, complete with Susan's command to hush and see what Aslan is doing, vividly parallels the creation scene in *Nephew*. Every door and window is thrown open to light and spring air as Aslan's spring enters the Witch's own abode. Aslan's breathing on the Witch's stone statues to bring them to life is similar to God's wind breathing on Ezekiel's valley of dry bones and making them live, in a fascinating narrative in Ezekiel 37.

What Can We Learn from Aslan?

From Aslan, we can learn the power of full forgiveness (there's no need to talk with Edmund about what is past).

Lucy is horrified at the Witch's claim on her brother's life and asks, "Can nothing be done to save Edmund?" "All shall be done," says

Aslan. "But it may be harder than you think." Aslan neither excuses nor condemns Peter when Peter takes some of the blame for Edmund going wrong, but merely looks at him.

A Child's-Eye View

Much in *Wardrobe* appeals to the senses: soft fur coats and Aslan's own fur, crunching snow, good food (and magical Turkish Delight), the quick blossoming and birdsong at the end of the Witch's enchanted winter—even the palpable sense of fear that the wolves will overtake the children and the beavers on the way to the Stone Table.

It's fun to watch the fast change from winter to spring, with descriptive passages and very specific details: the kinds of flowers (snowdrops, primroses, and many more), the looks of each type of tree (larches, birches, laburnums, beech trees). Many children love winter, but winter can seem endless, and seeing it end in a few hours would be wonderful after a hundred years of enduring it.

Of course, the main draw for children is Aslan himself: the good lion who is more powerful than the Witch, who cares enough to die for Edmund, who lets children play with him and ride him, and who is wise and good. We feel, reading *Wardrobe*, that we've been allowed to look into those solemn but gentle eyes, stroke that shaggy mane, and learn from the Lion.

Series-Wide Issues Lewis Develops

Lewis didn't know he would be writing a series when he penned this book. But he put in many elements and truths that he found worth revisiting in later books. He also included some bits of wisdom unique to this book.

Sayings and Sound Advice

Through the years, a few thousand children have probably checked out their wardrobes and closets for magic countries, just in case, after reading *Wardrobe*. So Lewis wisely emphasizes not to shut the wardrobe door when you go in it. (As the Professor says at the end of *Wardrobe*, Narnia can't be found through wardrobes anymore, anyway. Sorry.)

Navigating Narnia

A wardrobe with two doors from Lewis's childhood, made by his grandfather, is now housed at the Wade Center, Wheaton College (Wheaton, Illinois). The one in the Kilns (Lewis's adult home) had only one door and a looking glass (more like the description in *Wardrobe*)—now on display at Reynolds Hall at Westmont College in Santa Barbara. But wardrobes were merely a place to store clothes, and Lewis didn't necessarily need a specific model.

But of course, far more important than this piece of wisdom is what we learn about relationships with enemies—dealing with them and offering them opportunities to repent, but not letting them continue to hurt others if it is in our power to stop them.

Edmund's siblings are horrified at the thought of his going to the Witch's house. Thinking only of his safety, they want to go after him and rescue Edmund from her clutches. The beavers are wiser. They tell the children that they must keep away from the White Witch and go to Aslan. Lucy, in particular, learns this lesson well and learns to call directly to Aslan when she is in distress.

Narnian Themes

We learn in *Wardrobe*, "Once a king or queen in Narnia, always a king or queen in Narnia." That sets the stage for the Pevensies to travel back to Narnia, with Peter still being the high king, in later books.

When the children hesitate in the Narnian woods, Mr. Beaver tells them to come "further in." They must be committed to Narnia; they are actually necessary for the future of the land. For the next few years, England needs to be in their past.

As much as Edmund might like to think that his story that Narnia doesn't exist makes more sense than Lucy's story that both of them had been there, for the Professor, it boiled down to the question of which of the two was more truthful. In the days ahead in Narnia, reputation matters. It's important to choose the right side and to conduct oneself with integrity.

Narnia and our world are interdependent. Contact between Narnia and Earth is supernatural and mythical from both sides, as we see in *Wardrobe* and again in several other *Chronicles*. Elements of myth are shadows of a greater reality, and seeing the wonder of Earth through the eyes of Tumnus or King Caspian helps us see and appreciate our own wonderful world, which is charged with the grandeur God gave it.

Peter didn't feel brave when he went to kill the wolf, but he killed it anyway because it was his duty. Many times in the stories ahead, he and the other children will find their desires and their duties in conflict. Sometimes they make the right choice, and sometimes the wrong one. Aslan is often present to warn those who are considering the wrong choice (as when Edmund and Caspian argued at Deathwater Island, in *Voyage*, over which king had greater claims to an island that might make the claimant rich).

Religious References, Mythic Echoes

This tale of the forces of good and evil, and the voluntary death of one who is good, echoes grand themes from life and literature. In particular, it highlights the great love Jesus showed in His voluntary death for each one of us. *Wardrobe* also has numerous mythical and literary hints, so we'll look at each one quickly.

The White Witch is said to be descended from Lilith, a female demon in Babylonian and Hebrew myth, and the mythical first wife of Adam, the first man. *Wardrobe* thus pits the offspring of Adam and Eve (the Pevensie children) against those of Lilith.

The white stag the Pevensies hunt at the end (echoing a mention of it by Tumnus at the beginning) comes from Celtic lore and Hungarian myth, and indicates that one is about to cross into another world. Two brothers, Hunor and Magar, followed a white stag into Scythia and became two groups of people, the Huns and the Magyars.

Biblical Parallels

As one might expect in a story that parallels the crucifixion and resurrection of Jesus Christ, much in this story reflects biblical truth. The White Witch's accusations against Edmund are like Satan as accuser. (She has the role of Satan on several levels.) After Satan has succeeded in tempting someone, he accuses the person to God, hoping to get him or her punished.

Aslan didn't become incarnate as a lion in Narnia, as Jesus took on human flesh in addition to his nature as God. Aslan *is* a lion, from before the beginning of Narnia.

The Witch had reason to fear Aslan, knowing she deserved death at his paws. The Bible tells us that the rebellious unbeliever should also fear God, for "It is a fearful thing to fall into the hands of the living God" (Hebrews 10:31). As much as the Witch and Satan want to accuse their enemies, it is really God who does the judging.

The Deeper Magic is a voluntary sacrifice of a perfect victim. The killing of a perfect animal was the basis for a great deal of biblical history, including the Old Testament sacrificial system and the prophecies pointing to Jesus. Jesus took the place of those animal sacrifices. He lived a perfect life and then was killed as a perfect sacrifice. Jesus voluntarily submitted to a hideous death, including the horror of God the Father rejecting Him for some time because He carried our sins and God can't look at sin.

The emperor's magic is said to be written on the "fire-stones on the Secret Hill" or the roots of the world ash tree, depending on which edition you have, mentioned by the Witch in Chapter 13. (The world ash tree is the mythical Yggdrasil, which holds Earth together.) They are like the stone tablets of the Ten Commandments, written by God and given to Moses in Exodus 31:18.

When Edmund leaves during a meal to betray Aslan, we are reminded of Judas, the one of Jesus' 12 apostles who betrayed Jesus. He left during the Last Supper to go and betray Jesus for the price of 30 silver coins.

Greek and Roman

The Roman god Vertumnus often tricks maidens into coming to see his home and is thus probably the inspiration for Mr. Tumnus, who deceived Lucy Pevensie into going back to his cozy little cave with him. Ovid's long poem *Metamorphoses* tells of Vertumnus and his love for the beautiful but haughty Pomona, goddess of orchards. (He disguised himself as an old woman to trick her and suggested that she marry Vertumnus. It worked.)

Silenus, Pan's son, may be the first official satyr. He was the teacher and faithful companion of Bacchus. Tumnus is familiar with him and has the *Life and Letters of Silenus* on his bookshelf. Silenus is less mythical to Tumnus than humans are.

Arthurian

Aslan's temporary court at the Stone Table is marked with a yellow silk pavilion and the Lion's banner, making Aslan look much like a medieval king surrounded by courtiers. The speech patterns at the end of the book, showing how the grown-up Pevensies talk, are medieval and courtly.

Norse

Wolves are a big part of Norse mythology. The evil god Loki had a man-eating wolf for a son. Fenris Ulf was a great wolf of Scandinavian mythology.

Winter is significant in Norse mythology, too, as we might expect in a cold land. Scandinavia is named after Skadi, the goddess of winter. Wolves are sacred to Skadi, but she is just, not a prototype for the White Witch. Bestla, the frost giantess, is Odin's mother.

Navigating Narnia

Lewis made revisions throughout the *Chronicles* for the American edition. Among those, he renamed the White Witch's head wolf, Maugrim, calling him Fenris Ulf. But editions of the *Chronicles* published since 1994 reflect the earlier British wording.

Dropping Hints: Literary Allusions

Reflections of many of Lewis's favorite authors, and of Lewis's own life, come in *Wardrobe*, the most developed of his Narnia tales.

Professor Kirke is quite a fan of Plato and mentions him repeatedly, here and in *Battle*. The magical wardrobe has a looking glass in its door, perhaps a hint of *Alice in Wonderland*. And the mice chewing Aslan's cords are a nod to Aesop's fables, where a mouse returns a favor done by a lion (not eating the mouse when he has the chance) by chewing the lion's ropes and freeing him when he is captured by hunters.

But wait—there's more. Let's look at a few sources in a little more detail.

All Those Other Authors

One of the most obvious connections is the archetypal use of the snow queen. Hans Christian Andersen's snow queen, in the story with that title, has many parallels to Lewis's White Witch. In *The Snow Queen*, a boy named Kay encounters a regal woman in a sledge. She is dressed in white fur, tall and beautiful but cold and pale. Like Edmund, Kay is initially afraid but then enchanted, and willingly entrapped. Both boys must be rescued by someone who loves them.

Irene in MacDonald's *The Princess and the Goblin* may serve as a model for Lucy. Like Lucy, Irene finds mystery and magic, and a world others believe to be make-believe. Irene goes up several long staircases and finds her fairy grandmother, but others don't believe her tale until they themselves have seen proof. Her friend Curdie is particularly skeptical, like Lucy's older siblings, but like the Professor, Curdie's mother insists that the honest young girl deserves to be believed.

In another of MacDonald's books, *Phantastes*, one of the most important books in Lewis's life as noted in Chapter 1, one lady was rescued out of marble, akin to the reviving of the many statues in *Wardrobe*. MacDonald also wrote *Lilith*, a book based on the mythical figure Lilith, who is the White Witch's ancestor according to Mr. Beaver.

When Aslan asks the children and the newly revived former statues to search in the Witch's castle for statues, he tells them to look "upstairs and downstairs, and in my lady's chamber"—a quote from nursery rhyme "Goosey, Goosey, Gander."

In E. Nesbit's book *The Amulet*, five children traveled back in time. However many days they visited another time, only minutes had passed when they returned—an idea Lewis used repeatedly in Narnia.

Reflections of Lewis's Writings and Life

During World War II, the Lewis brothers hosted school children in the Kilns, as did many others who lived in safer areas outside the big cities. His visitors during the war provided a good starting place for child visitors exploring a large, unfamiliar house.

The Professor's housekeeper, Mrs. Macready, was probably named after the housekeeper from Lewis's own boyhood, Mrs. McCreedy.

When an American school girl wrote to him for writing advice, his December 14, 1959, reply to her (printed in the 1993 edition of his collected *Letters of C. S. Lewis*), gives several pieces of advice that Lewis himself followed. Here are a few of his tips: Read all the good books you can. Write for the ear, not the eye. Write about what really interests you. Be clear.

The Least You Need to Know

- *The Lion, the Witch and the Wardrobe* was the first of the *Chronicles* published, and it was written to be a single book, not the beginning of a series.

- The Pevensie children make it into Narnia through a wardrobe and find themselves confronted by a prophecy that they will be its kings and queens; two or more Pevensies are present in five of the seven *Chronicles*.

- Aslan rescued the land from the White Witch who had been its evil ruler for a hundred years, and he died and came to life again to free Edmund from the White Witch's claim on his life.

Chapter 8

Prince Caspian: The Return to Narnia

In This Chapter

- The introduction of Prince/King Caspian
- Restoring Old Narnia from years of being in hiding
- A good look at several individual talking beasts and other creatures
- A second visit to Narnia for the Pevensie children

More than a thousand years have passed since the Pevensies ruled in Narnia's Golden Age. Much has changed. The woods have gone silent, and the land is completely under the rule of men. Whether the talking beasts exist at all is a matter of speculation; the period in which they roamed is now called "Old Narnia," and many refuse to believe that they or Aslan ever existed.

But Prince Caspian loves the tales of Old Narnia, and it is within his power to awaken it. To do so, he will need help; he is but a boy, and war seems inevitable. Susan's horn, blown by Caspian, summons the Pevensies into Narnia to help with this new threat to the land's existence and the proper rule over it.

Fast Facts

This second book begins with exactly the same words as *Wardrobe*, an introduction to the four children. The subtitle (*Return to Narnia*) is the only place *Narnia* appears in the book titles, although several of Lewis's first title choices included the name. Lewis said many reported that they like *Caspian* least in the series. (That is also the vote of Cheryl's 8-year-old nephew, Ezekiel.)

Caspian looks at faith in an age of unbelief. What is sufficient evidence for belief? How do different beings respond to evidence? Where does mythology interact with truth? The ancient legend of Susan's horn and the tales of Narnia's Golden Age come to life as Old Narnia is revived and restored.

Navigating Narnia

Caspian is dedicated to Mary Clare Havard, daughter of Dr. R. E. "Humphrey" Havard (Robert was his real name). Mary's father was Lewis's physician and a member of the Inklings (see Chapter 1).

This time the Pevensies come to Narnia not to rule, but to install Caspian on his throne. A significant part of *Caspian*'s most important action is told as a flashback—a story recounted by Trumpkin the dwarf to bring the Pevensies up to speed on where Narnia now stands and why they might be needed in Narnia.

Who Will We Meet?

Because many years have gone by in Narnia, only the visitors and Aslan himself will seem familiar from *Wardrobe*. Narnia has undergone drastic changes, which we see largely through the eyes of old friends, the Pevensies.

The Pevensies (Arriving by Train)

The children are called into Narnia, and they find the summoning physically uncomfortable—they feel like they're being dragged and pulled. Edmund realizes it is magic, and he exhorts them to hold hands. This is a genie-being-summoned story in reverse, told from the perspective of the genie.

It takes a while for the children to recognize Cair Paravel because it has changed so greatly, and even longer to confirm their tentative identification of their old palace. When they take the gifts they received from Father Christmas, they wish Susan's horn were there so they could take it. Ironically, that very horn is what called them, so, of course, it isn't in the chamber.

On their journey by foot with the dwarf Trumpkin, nobody is able to know precisely where to go, as even the river has changed course a bit in the past thousand-plus years of Narnia. Aslan appears to Lucy, but the others don't believe she has seen him, and they lose time going another way. At his second appearance, he tells Lucy she is to follow him alone, if necessary. The others reluctantly follow.

Lucy's call by Aslan in the middle of the night is similar to the prophet Samuel's call by God as a child, in 1 Samuel 3. Samuel had to be called three times, Lucy twice—but Lucy knew it was Aslan the first time, and Samuel didn't know at first that it was God calling him.

The Stone Table has long since been covered by a mound called Aslan's How. Going inside it, the boys are overwhelmed by wall carvings that look old, although the children themselves are "older." In effect, by going back and forth between Narnia and Earth, the children have become time travelers in Narnia, moving through many generations of Narnian history in a single year on Earth.

God Sightings

Aslan wants the children to obey even if they don't see him. They are asked to walk by faith. Sometimes Christians can clearly see what God wants. Other times we have to read Scripture, get wise counsel, and then move forward only one step at a time, waiting for guidance on the next step.

Peter sends a letter to Miraz challenging him to single combat, as one knight to another. Miraz doesn't believe in the High King of Narnia (he thinks the old tales are nursery stories for babies) and isn't inclined to risk his stronger position on single combat. But Miraz's men goad him into accepting it. The battle still must be fought, even with the usurper dead, because Miraz's men seek his throne.

At the end of *Caspian*, the older two are told they can't return to Narnia. They don't tell the others what Aslan has said to them. We hear what Aslan tells the younger two, in *Voyage*, when they themselves are told they cannot return. The fact that Peter will be able to return to the *new* Narnia someday, in *Battle*, remains a secret.

Navigating Narnia

Funny things happen to the children's ages. First they grow up in Narnia, and then they return to England as children again. When they return to Narnia now, they are children. Lewis said that age doesn't matter as much as people think. In a letter published in *Letters to Children*, he says that at 12 and at 50 both, parts of him are 12 and parts are 50.

Prince Caspian and His Household

When Prince Caspian is first introduced, his family members include his uncle, Miraz, who is the king of Narnia, and Miraz's wife, Prunaprismia. The royal couple have no children, so the king is willing to train Caspian as the heir for the throne. (Once a son is born, things change in a hurry, so try to take your coffee break before that.) Prince Caspian also has a nanny, who tells him stories of Old Narnia, the time when the trees and beasts talked.

Caspian really should be king; his uncle is a usurper, but Caspian doesn't know it. He is descended from the first Caspian, known as Caspian the Conqueror. (Our Caspian is Caspian X.) Many nobles have been killed by his uncle or sent into hiding. As a result of this heritage, creatures in Old Narnia initially have a hard time trusting Caspian.

After a life of royal luxury, Caspian is enchanted by the simpler pleasures of sleeping under the stars, drinking well water, and eating nuts and wild fruits. His light-hearted spirit soon meets reality, however—if he is to survive, and Old Narnia with him, war is ahead. Caspian is shy about meeting the old kings from the Golden Age of Narnia, ancient history. He is in over his head as they arrive, dealing with a traitor and two unsavory characters that have been brought into Aslan's How. (He is bitten by a werewolf in the ensuing chaos, but apparently nothing comes of the bite, because he himself never seems to howl at a full moon.) He needs the help of kings and queens who have been little more than legends to him, to fight beings who were only mythical to the Pevensies before their first trip to Narnia.

Caspian will be king under Peter the High King, according to Aslan (leading to an argument between Edmund and Caspian in *Voyage* as to which of them is the higher king). After success in battle, Peter knights Caspian, and Caspian honors those who have fought bravely.

Doctor Cornelius

Doctor Cornelius, Prince Caspian's tutor, also knows the stories of Old Narnia, but he dares not tell them openly. (Caspian's nurse was dismissed for doing so.) Caspian is glad to learn the old stories are true, even if those days are past.

The tutor is a wise, ugly, kind person with merry eyes; though he is a half-dwarf, he himself has seen only glimpses of Old Narnia. Doctor Cornelius seeks an opportunity to tell his student of Narnia's true history and his role in it. He also teaches Caspian sword-fighting, riding, swimming, archery, music, hunting, and various academic disciplines.

Doctor Cornelius knows what Caspian does not—that Old Narnia is still in existence, and that someday Caspian will be its rescuer. He knows he is preparing Caspian for a life of war against his own family and everything he has known. When the day comes that Caspian must flee or be killed because a new prince has been born, Doctor Cornelius tells him his danger ... and the rest of the story—including the relevant information that he is the rightful king, Caspian X, and that only he can save Narnia at this crucial hour.

Schooling in Narnia is not generally shown to be a good thing. Only this education, one on one training under a tutor, seems good, in honor of Lewis's own pleasant days of learning under a good tutor rather than in the schools he hated.

Badgers and Dwarfs and Bears (Oh My)

Prince Caspian has heard of the talking beasts and dwarfs, but has never seen any. In a whirlwind of introductions, he meets dwarfs, a loyal talking badger, the Bulgy Bears (one of whom sucks his paw), dancing fauns, a loyal but stupid giant, and many other creatures who have been in hiding during the reigns of his ancestors. Most quickly accept him as the legitimate heir to the throne and a friend of Old Narnia.

Badgers are known for their tenacity; Trufflehunter is loyal and true. He rejoices in a good man being made king; he states that Narnia is the country of the talking beasts, but a man should rule it. The talking beasts are happiest when in their proper place of authority: under the king, but helping to care for the land and the mute beasts. The other alternatives, hiding or rebelling, aren't pleasant ones.

The dwarfs are harder to win. Skeptics by nature, dwarfs often end up being independent and cynical, or openly choosing the wrong side. Trumpkin needs to *see* everything before he will believe. The dwarfs at the smithy ask questions and hesitate to believe, but once they trust Caspian, they furnish valuable gifts of armor and weaponry.

The dwarf Nikabrik, on the other hand, is more and more unwilling to trust his companions and the young king. He is willing to call up the White Witch and deal with ogres and hags—and finally he chooses open defiance and treason. Whoever will get rid of the Telmarines, that's who he is willing to support. He could go either way—believing in Aslan or not—but he's not willing to wait around if Aslan doesn't act on his timetable. Ultimately he cares more about his own comfort than about what is right, and he loses any chance to experience what is good.

Only in wise submission to one's proper role—whether that role is that of a king or one with less authority and less responsibility—can any of Narnia's characters find peace and happiness. Aslan has set up a world, like ours, in which authority structures are in place for the guidance and safety of those being ruled. Hebrews 13:17 instructs us to obey authority because those who hold authority are responsible to God; we can make their responsibility easier and more joyful if we obey.

Brave Reepicheep

A small contingent of warriors presents itself to the young king. He hides his amusement but doesn't really expect much from Reepicheep and his followers. (We did mention that Reepicheep and his fellow warriors are mice, didn't we?) Even Aslan is impressed by the love Reepicheep's followers have for him.

Reepicheep, like all the smaller breeds of talking animals, is much larger than an average mouse. The books are a little inconsistent here. Descriptions vary from well over a foot to more than 2 feet. It's probably hard to get a mouse to stand still long enough to measure him.

> **Magic and Myth**
>
> In the loving development of Reepicheep's character, it's not hard to see that Lewis actually enjoyed mice—a fact he readily admitted. He left out bread crumbs for mice in his home, to entice them out so he could watch them. Beatrix Potter had much to do with his love for these cheeky little rodents. *That Hideous Strength* also showcases mice.

But Reepicheep is brave far beyond his size. We'll get a much better look at him in *Voyage*, but even in *Caspian* we can see that he is very courageous.

The Dwarf Trumpkin

Dwarfs are skeptics by nature. They are practical folks with deep connections to the earth. Having longer lives than men, they do not quickly change allegiances. Trumpkin has heard the tales of Aslan and the old kings and queens, but he doesn't believe them—any more than the men in Narnia at that point in its history believe in the existence of dwarfs. But he does believe when they are proven to him; he's an agnostic, but an honest one, who is willing to be proven wrong.

For all his doubt, Trumpkin is loyal and true. Once he determines to follow Caspian, he is willing to suffer, if required. Although he believes in neither the horn nor the help it might bring (Aslan or the four children), he volunteers to set off to the castle of Cair Paravel if his king wishes. It's not faith for him when he finally does believe in the horn, the Pevensie children, and Aslan, because he must see them with his own eyes. But he's willing to obey *before he sees proof.*

Later, traveling with the Pevensies, he says that if the traveling party splits up, he will go with the High King, as that is his duty. He never lets his doubts stand in the way of appropriate actions, nor does he cling to his doubts when he sees the truth. He is an *honest* skeptic.

His humility is on display after the Pevensies have proven to him that they are more than mere children. He thanks them for his life, his cure, his breakfast, and his lesson. When face to face with Aslan, finally made to believe, he has sense enough to go to him rather than flee.

Trumpkin proves such a faithful friend to Narnia that he is left at the castle as regent when Caspian sails on his long voyage looking for the seven lost lords in *Voyage*. By being responsible when he didn't have any authority, he earned the privilege of authority. The Bible says, "He that is faithful in that which is least is faithful also in much" (Luke 16:10 KJV), and Trumpkin is a perfect example of that truth.

Aslan Himself (in Glimpses at First)

Major changes have taken place in Narnia, and Aslan is needed to restore the land to its proper functioning order. But this time restoration comes from the bottom up: first the talking beasts are brought out of hiding, along with the dwarfs and other creatures. The Pevensie children are called into Narnia. Then Aslan shows up—but in puzzling half-glimpses. At first only Lucy sees him.

Lucy is surprised to find that Aslan seems bigger; Aslan tells her it is because she is older. When she asks is it not because he is older, he answers, "I am not." He is ageless—a hint that he stands outside Narnian time and is not bound by it.

The task he gives Lucy—to follow alone if she must—is a difficult one, but she will not be alone; she will be with him. After Lucy, Edmund is the first to see him (seeing his shadow before he sees Aslan himself) because he has been willing to follow on Lucy's word alone, and the others follow only reluctantly. Lucy's eyes were on Aslan, and the others on her—a picture of the Christian life.

Aslan's roar finally awakens the wood. The animals love him and rub against him, and Lucy and Susan are able to ride on his back again.

When Aslan gives the Telmarines freedom to leave Narnia, he tells them their history—our chance to see Aslan himself as a storyteller.

Dryads

Throughout the recent history of Narnia, the trees have been alive, but their dryads have been asleep. From the Telmarines' fear of the sea (Aslan comes across it) and the woods, they have allowed the land near Cair Paravel to grow wild and eventually to go to sleep.

The trees are very important to *Caspian*. The presence of dryads allows a fuller representation of nature as *alive* and infused with life by its creator—the medieval picture of nature as a dance, not a machine. The Telmarine soldiers believe the woods to be haunted by ghosts and are afraid of them. Thus, they have silenced them. When the trees are awakened, it is a sign that Aslan's land is about to be fully restored (like the end of the Witch's winter in *Wardrobe*).

Forests are very common in fairy tales, usually as dangerous places in which one can get lost or meet enemies. Think of Hansel and Gretel, Snow White, and Little Red Riding Hood. Fangorn Forest also plays a role in *The Lord of the Rings*, as a place of mystery and power.

Each tree species' dryads can be recognized: pale birch girls, queenly beeches, shaggy oak men, willow women with long hair and serious faces. They move not by walking on top of the soil, but through it, like wading through water.

Caspian, as a Telmarine, isn't automatically a friend of the trees. They are suspicious of him. But as the Pevensie children return to Narnia, the trees get gradually more and more wakeful (nearly coming awake when Lucy summons them), and finally coming fully awake and dancing for Aslan. When they enter the war, the Telmarines' fear makes the dryads a formidable enemy, and the war is all but won.

Dryads, who are very crucial to this story, come from Greek mythology, as do naiads (water nymphs). Most dryads are good, though many of the references to them in Narnia admit that a few are on the wrong side. Dryads die when their trees die, and *Caspian* shows that they can also slumber.

What Should We Watch For?

Very little of this book is fast paced; through most of the story, there is time to take in what is happening. But Narnia is a very different place than when we last saw it, so do be sure to keep your eyes open.

Navigating Narnia

Have you ever noticed the narrator of the *Chronicles*? His voice isn't intrusive or obvious, but from time to time, a first-person narrator interjects his own comment or advice. He even tells us he has spoken to Lucy. Here is a sample comment from *Wardrobe:* "I hope you know what I mean by a voice sounding pale." Watch for him.

Great Change in Narnia

More than 1,000 years have gone by since the Pevensies ruled in Narnia. Stories of their reign abound, along with tales of talking trees and other elements of magic, and a lion named Aslan. But the stories are whispered in secret, for the land is ruled by men, and there is no evidence the stories are true.

Cair Paravel has long since fallen into disuse, the Stone Table has been covered over (it is now Aslan's How), and the Fords of Beruna now have a bridge. (And unfortunately, beavers seem to be extinct in Narnia.) Think Rip Van Winkle had it bad, sleeping for 30 years and awakening to a changed world? Imagine an entire millennium passing in a land you once knew, while you grow only a year older. That is what the Pevensies experience. Their reign is now ancient history, Narnia's "Golden Age."

Who Can Be Trusted

Some in this story prove not to be friends of Narnia, so be cautious. Others will be much truer friends than seems possible at a first look.

Caspian is shocked to discover that the horrid creatures such as ogres and hags from Old Narnia also have descendants, not just the good ones. And some creatures could go either way. Caspian matures quickly as he learns discernment and leadership.

Creatures of a Delightful Variety

Caspian shows us more of the personalities and everyday lives of many of Narnia's citizens, long kept in hiding under unfriendly rule. Talking beasts include a badger, bears, mice, squirrels, and many other creatures. Dwarfs, fauns, giants, centaurs, and even a hag and a werewolf make appearances. The dryads (tree people) awaken from their long sleep, and the party is completed by Bacchus and many of his friends bringing refreshments. Lewis has tamed them considerably from their usual mythic identities.

The fauns on Dancing Lawn are mournful and merry at the same time. Caspian is delighted to see them, and they accept him as their king immediately upon finding out who he is.

And Narnia feels like itself again by the time of the magic dance of plenty, with food for all tastes, including the trees (who are served special soils for each course).

Unannounced School Vacations

Narnia has settled into an unpleasant era, and that means unpleasant schools. Watch for the unique ways Aslan shuts down two schools (one for boys and one for girls) near the end of the book.

Aslan's coming brings freedom to all. As always in Narnia, freedom doesn't mean the ability to break laws and hurt others, but the end of the story is the breaking of fetters for man and beast. Even Caspian's nurse, who seems to be on her deathbed, has her bed effectively moved into the free open air before Aslan heals her.

A Child's-Eye View

From a child's perspective, one of the best features of this tale may be the well-developed personalities of the talking beasts. We have wonderful individual looks at their homes or their way of life and their hospitality, such as the Bulgy Bears' gift of honey and Pattertwig's nut. We see creatures at work and play, dancing and eating. It's a long wait until we get to see Old Narnia, but once we do, we see it at its best and most alive.

Children will also enjoy Trumpkin's comeuppances when he tries to treat the Pevensies as cute little children. Bacchus (the Roman god of wine) and his maids might be a little puzzling, because children's stories don't tend to use them. Many children will rejoice with the boys and girls who get let out of school, and wonder when the Lion might be visiting their schools.

Series-Wide Issues Lewis Develops

Caspian focuses on the reestablishment of the proper relationship between Narnian people and other beings. Caspian, Aslan, and the Pevensies all have their roles in returning things to their proper places. In the Pevensies' return, we see the seriousness of the principle that a king or queen in Narnia is always a king or queen in Narnia. When they are needed, they are brought back.

Sayings and Sound Advice

The children find themselves in an unfamiliar place, and they are careful to make wise choices that will help them survive—including the choice not to try to swim away from the island, because they do not know the water.

Lucy realized one of the best ways to get to sleep on a sleepless night is to stop trying.

When Nikabrik despises Dr. Cornelius for his heritage, being a half-dwarf, Trufflehunter wisely tells him that no one is responsible for his ancestry. Racial superiority can destroy Narnia quickly, if it is tolerated, and it is not.

Narnian Themes

Feasting, celebrating, and romping are essential in Narnia. For a long time now, most of Narnia has been under the rule of people who live a very practical life that doesn't include feasting and dancing, while Old Narnia has been in exile. It's appropriate, then, that the book starts out with many references to lack of food, for the Pevensies and others.

Initially, they have two lunches for four children, and then for several days they live on apples and water. But by the end, fasting has turned to feasting, exile has turned to celebration, and hiding has been replaced with dancing.

Each creature does what he does best, the Narnian principle for unity in diversity. Glenstorm the centaur says it is the job of himself and his sons to watch, the badger's to remember.

Trumpkin isn't sure he believes in Aslan, but he is wise enough to believe his own eyes. And like others in the series, on first meeting Aslan he understands without being told that going to Aslan, not running away, is the wise thing to do. Trumpkin is the only character in the series that the Lion pounces on, but for this character who only believes what he sees and hears, perhaps a lion's jaws and paws are necessary for full belief. And in the end, he does believe and trusts fully in Aslan's goodness.

As is common in the *Chronicles*, those who have been defeated but are not utterly corrupt are offered mercy: the Telmarines are free to leave or stay. Some are willing to be part of Narnia under the new regime, where the animals are as important as they are. Others prefer to return to our land, where people are in charge. It is up to them.

Religious References, Mythic Echoes

Caspian doesn't have nearly as many mythical hints as *Wardrobe*, but Lewis still borrowed from other stories. Let's look at a few.

Biblical Parallels

Caspian had wanted a better heritage than being a descendant of pirates, so Aslan told him he was ultimately descended from the Lord Adam and Lady Eve—honor and shame both. The honor comes from the fact that Adam and Eve, and thus all their descendants, were made in God's image. The shame comes from their choice to disobey God and bring sin on all their descendants, told in Genesis 3.

The restoration of Narnia to the land it is supposed to be can be likened to the restoration of Israel, its wall, and its temple, in the paired books of Ezra and Nehemiah in the Old Testament.

Greek and Roman

The tearing down of the Bridge of Beruna was similar to Bacchus's destruction of a ship in Ovid's *Metamorphosis*, Book 3. Bromios and the Ram were other names for Bacchus, who is traditionally greeted with a shout of "Euan, euan, eu-oi-oi-oi."

The Roman goddess Pomona (who is described as the greatest of the wood people) put good spells on the apple orchard that the moles planted when the Pevensies still ruled at Cair Paravel. She is generally associated with the blossoming of trees.

Arthurian

Peter's single combat is the proper kind of warfare for a medieval knight. This knight is no longer the young boy Peter, but once again the proven warrior Sir Peter Wolf's-Bane, the name given to him when Aslan knights him in *Wardrobe* (called Fenris-Bane in some editions). His duel is conducted honorably, under the rules of chivalry—not taking unfair advantage if an opponent trips, for example. In contrast, the other side isn't honorable, and Miraz's own people do away with him.

Norse

The Vikings invented the game that became chess, and their mythology includes golden chessmen belonging to the gods. Susan is distressed by her discovery of a golden knight, its eyes two little rubies (one of them missing), because she remembered their good times long ago in Narnia.

Dropping Hints: Literary Allusions

Most of *Caspian* seems to be based on the logical results of known story lines: the likely actions of a traitorous king, the personality a talking badger would have, dwarfs confronted with evidence that challenges their prior experience, and the Pevensies returning to a land that is partly familiar and yet mostly unfamiliar. Lewis relied on basic rules of warfare and historical probabilities, probably more than he relied on other books. Still, we see hints of other authors.

All Those Other Authors

When a magician in *Arabian Nights*, such as Aladdin, calls the jinn (genie), it has no choice but to come. And so the Pevensie children are summoned from our world, and Susan recognizes that their experience is like that jinn.

Throughout *Caspian*, we have *foreshadowings* of what will happen when the trees come fully alive, and hints that they are beginning to do so. The Telmarines' terror when the tree people join the battle hints of the fear of Shakespeare's Macbeth. Macbeth had felt himself safe because of prophecies he had interpreted in his own favor.

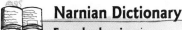

Narnian Dictionary

Foreshadowing is an author's hint to pay attention to a specific plot element that will be important later in the story. One method of foreshadowing is repeated use of one element, such as *Caspian*'s references to the dryads and the Telmarines' fear of the trees.

One of those was his danger when the Birnam wood would come to Dunisnane—a prophecy that seemed impossible. But when his enemies cut down trees and carried them to Dunisnane, it looked like the woods were indeed moving, and Macbeth knew his doom was near.

Reflections of Lewis's Writings and Life

Lewis was a great hiker and greatly loved creation and animal life. In *Caspian*, Susan's horn could have brought the children to the very place of the battle. By bringing them to Cair Paravel instead, Lewis interspersed enough time for a good long hike in which the children could be updated by Trumpkin, rather than finding themselves suddenly transported to Narnia in the midst of a battle.

The Least You Need to Know

- *Prince Caspian* is the first of three books that take place during the life and reign of Caspian X (the others: *Voyage* and *Chair*).

- *Caspian* focuses on returning Narnia to its rightful workings, a kingdom where man is king but talking beasts are free citizens.

- The Pevensie children return to Narnia because they are needed; as kings and queens of Narnia, they still have a duty there when their presence is necessary.

Chapter 9

The Voyage of the Dawn Treader

In This Chapter

- A voyage to find the seven lords banished by Caspian's uncle Miraz

- Visits to lands in the outlying regions of Narnian rule—and beyond charted waters, to the utter east

- The transformation of Eustace Scrubb

Imagine the opportunity to set sail on a king's errand, with a talking mouse and other brave friends, traveling to islands no one is sure exist. Given such a chance, it's probably better to leave your bratty cousin at home.

What would you want to see? Dragons, underwater towns, sea serpents? How about invisible enemies, dark lands where nightmares come true, slave traders, and men lying in a seven-year nap? Would you rather stay home? Too late. The voyage is underway. Hang on to your hat—and please stop your cousin before he tries to fight with that mouse.

Because the *Dawn Treader* is sailing beyond waters and islands on Narnian maps, we get to be in on the discovery of uncharted territories. Some are frightening places, and the voyage doesn't always go smoothly. Most of the voyagers don't see Aslan at all on this trip. But glimpses of his provision and his guidance show up frequently, and he himself is present at the end, for those from our world.

Fast Facts

King Caspian sets out on a voyage to discover the seven good lords banished by his evil uncle Miraz during Miraz's illegal rule; it's a dangerous but rewarding journey to what might be the edge of the world.

This book was written in less than three months and published in 1952. Remember Lucy Barfield, the dedicatee of *Wardrobe? Voyage* is dedicated to Lucy's foster brother, Geoffrey Barfield.

Since the Pevensies' last visit, we have had one year Earth time, three Narnian—the shortest distance between tales.

Stylistically, *Voyage* is different from the other *Chronicles* because it is multiple episodes rather than one straight story. It also takes place completely outside the borders of Narnia, although the Lone Islands (visited in the first part of the voyage) come under Narnian sovereignty.

Who Will We Meet?

Voyage's door from Earth into Narnia is an unusual one, neither train station nor literal door. This time, three children from our world are drawn in through a painting of a Narnian ship, which turns out to be Caspian's *Dawn Treader*, already at sea for 30 days when we join up with them. So let's make sure we understand the reasons for this voyage before we get on board: besides Caspian's purpose of sailing to find the seven banished lords, Reepicheep the mouse especially wants to go as far east as they can sail, hoping to find Aslan's own country.

Eustace Clarence Scrubb

Voyage's very first sentence, one of the most famous lines in the *Chronicles*, warns us that Eustace, the Pevensies' cousin, is trouble. It pays to keep our eyes on this boy. He doesn't want to be on a tiny little ship with a talking mouse, and he insists on being sent back to the British Consulate. Unfortunately, Narnia doesn't seem to have embassies, so he's stuck—and we're stuck with him.

Eustace seems to be an exaggeration of Lewis's own boyhood. Lewis describes himself as a "prig" during his boarding-school days. Although he was bullied rather than a bully, he thought himself superior to his classmates. Useless (sorry, we meant *Eustace*) continually complains about any deprivations or perceived hardship, especially about working. When the ship docks at an island so that its people can make necessary repairs, he looks for a place to hide to get out of work. The others on the *Dawn Treader* have to end a long day of hard work putting together a search party for a useless member of the team.

Magic and Myth

The water at the end of the voyage is sweet, no longer salty. It is strong enough to quench thirst and hunger, and to allow them to look directly at the sun. It even makes the old men a little bit younger. It seems to be the fountain of youth, searched for in many tales.

Eustace, meanwhile, is in a valley that seems to have only one treacherous exit. The valley has burned patches in the grass, a hint to the reader that there's danger afoot. And that danger soon proves to be a fire-breathing dragon—or, rather, a smoke-breathing, nearly dead dragon. It dies in Eustace's presence.

Eustace thinks dragonish thoughts in a dragon's cave, which proves to be a dangerous indulgence. A dragon himself when he wakes, he eats the dead dragon (ewww!) and flies out of the valley. Unlike most boys, the narrator tells us, Eustace hadn't thought much about treasure, or dragons, or adventure. But he *had* thought about his own desires; although the adventure of a dragon's treasure hoard had never occurred to him, he was quickly attracted by the wealth it represented.

The idea of a person being turned into a creature is an old one in literature; from Pinocchio turning into a donkey (because of his laziness) to a prince turning into a bear in the fairy tale *East of the Sun and West of the Moon*. In George MacDonald's *The Princess and Curdie*, human beings who've made bad choices are turned into beasts, sometimes quite hideous ones, but can turn back into human beings through wiser actions as beasts.

As a dragon, Eustace is a nuisance, and knows it, and is sorry instead of glad, a sign that he is not the same boy. (Well, duh, he's not the same boy—he is huge and scaly, breathes fire, and eats raw meat!) And now Eustace has a brand-new pleasure: liking others and being liked.

Edmund and Lucy

Peter and Susan are too old for Narnia now, but Edmund and Lucy are not. It seems rather unfortunate for them that their cousin, Eustace, is their traveling companion on this visit (which proves to be their own last visit). By the way, this is the only book in the *Chronicles* in which the number of boy and girl visitors is not kept even. All others have one boy and one girl, or two of each. Eustace is the "odd" man.

The first night at sea, Lucy is nearly too happy to speak, at the joy of being back in Narnia. She loves the adventure of sailing to unknown lands, possibly to Aslan's own country.

Lucy shows her usual kindness when she knows the dragon is Eustace, by getting up her courage and kissing its face. This is much like the character Elsie kissing a dragon on its forehead in E. Nesbit's story "Justnowland" from *The Magic World*. Edmund has his own chance at kindness when he is alone with the newly undragoned Eustace, and quickly tells him that he himself was worse on his first trip to Narnia because he was a traitor.

Lucy also has to be very brave in taking on the role of magician's assistant and making the monopods visible again, on the magician's island. But there she also faces great temptation—the desire to be prettier than her sister, even if it hurts others. Such a temptation goes against her usual desire to help others, and suggests deeper conflict with Susan than we see on the surface.

King Caspian

Prince Caspian is now King Caspian. Narnia is well established under Caspian, and faithful Trumpkin the dwarf is left at home as regent while Caspian is at sea. It's time to right one last wrong the Narnians suffered under "King" Miraz: the banishment of the seven lords who served faithfully under Caspian's father. Equipped only with the lords' names and the fact that they sailed beyond the Lone Islands, Caspian sets out to find them. To do so, he will enter uncharted waters and possibly risk the lives of himself and his crew.

The voyage has been underway 30 days and is coming near the Lone Islands when three children arrive to join the trip, splashing magically in the waters near the ship rather than arriving on shipboard.

The stops at various islands remind some readers of the *Odyssey*, but actually the book has more in common with the medieval legend of St. Brendan's voyage to the Land of Promise. St. Brendan is Ireland's most notable saint and perhaps its most adventurous, called Brendan the Navigator. Like *Voyage*, this tale includes a journey seeking paradise, three latecomers to the journey, a sea monster, and more.

Voyage is our best look at a Narnian king's daily interactions with his subjects. Caspian is young and sometimes impetuous, but in this book we see his growing wisdom and ability to take advice. He welcomes Lord Bern's idea for giving a show of power to Governor Gumpas, in signals to imaginary "other ships." For his wisdom and loyalty, Lord Bern is made the Duke.

> **Navigating Narnia**
>
> Lord Bern is an honorable man. He has proven faithful when not being watched and is given greater responsibility. He proves extremely useful to Caspian: buying him from slavery, reporting the condition of the islands, and counseling him wisely. Caspian shows his own wisdom in listening to an older man and taking his advice.

One of Caspian's greatest shows of wisdom is the offer of a cask of wine to celebrate his visit, when the soldiers need to decide quickly whether to welcome him or treat him as an enemy. Toward the end of the voyage, when the travelers are tired, discouraged, and a little bit afraid of traveling to the unnavigated end of the world, Caspian revives their courage by presenting the trip to the end of the world as a feat and an honor, complete with riches and a title to be bestowed on each traveler and his descendants. He has learned how to motivate people by finding their deepest desires and appealing to those—and by doing that, he proves to be a wise leader who knows the people under his leadership.

Reepicheep

Reepicheep's valor has been well proved in battle. Since he was a baby mouse in his cradle, he has longed for the utter east, believing it to be the way to Aslan's country. Reepicheep is focused—he wants to get to the utter east and to explore everything on the way.

Reepicheep is a fully developed character of this book and the favorite Narnian character of many readers, next to Aslan. Reepicheep is the exact opposite of self-centered, whiny, cowardly Eustace, and the two have inevitable conflict. Eustace even swings Reep by his tail and is rewarded by strikes from the flat of Reepicheep's sword. We are told it felt like a birch rod, a new experience for Eustace: a suggestion that he is an undisciplined brat who has never been spanked, although he has often deserved to be.

At any rate, Reepicheep readily offers friendship once Eustace is open to receiving it. (Before anyone knows the dragon is an enchanted human, Reepicheep has to be told not to fight the dragon. Truly he has more courage than sense at times!)

Navigating Narnia

Lewis said, in a letter to a child, that anyone who spends his whole life longing for heaven will be like Reepicheep. Reepicheep was honorable, of good reputation, and brave. He didn't fear death; in fact, he longed for it. Though that sometimes made him act foolishly, generally it gave him courage. Death was just the door to Aslan's country and not to be feared as, for the Christian, death is the door to being with Jesus in heaven.

Reepicheep's risk-taking is so great that if he forgets himself when playing chess, he deliberately endangers his chess men, taking them into risky positions he himself would take in real life. Reepicheep often acts first, thinks later. His instinctive actions are based on bravery and loyalty. He's much like Jesus' apostle Peter in that regard. Peter even used his sword to chop off an ear of someone in the crowd coming to arrest Jesus (John 18:10)! We're guessing he wasn't really aiming at the guy's ear; he just swung the sword, and the ear got in the way.

The crew lacks courage as they face an area of utter darkness, and they enter only because Reepicheep considers their hesitation cowardly. Entering the darkness doesn't seem a wise or useful thing to do, but Reepicheep reminds them that they are on an adventure, and this is a true adventure. Nevertheless, a lord awaits desperately in the darkness, frantic for rescue from the land where dreams—nightmares—come true. And rescuing the lords was the purpose of the voyage. So Reepicheep's "senseless" bravery ends up advancing the crew's goal after all.

Lord Drinian

Lord Drinian is the *Dawn Treader*'s captain. He summarizes the trip to date for the newly arrived travelers and welcomes them aboard. They have been traveling for nearly 30 days and are more than 400 leagues from Narnia. They hope to reach the Lone Islands in two days, but after the Lone Islands, the sea hasn't been charted.

Lord Drinian is a proven friend of Caspian's in *Voyage*, where tragedy will nearly destroy their friendship. But they have sailed together and proved each other, and they remain friends.

The Lost Lords

One by one, we meet the lost lords—or see what happened to them. We won't give all the details, but here are a few points:

- Lord Restimar remembered Caspian's father and proved a very useful friend to Caspian; he is made duke of the Lone Islands when the governor proves resistant to his Narnian emperor.

- Lord Octesian had an encounter with a very, very large reptile.

- Lord Restimar was, by the time the crew discovered him, worth his weight in gold.

- Lord Rhoop decided to give up a life of dreaming.

- Lords Revilian, Argoz, and Mavramorn were waiting quietly for the *Dawn Treader* and its crew.

Aslan

Aslan appears in this book in several forms, and as himself only briefly, before the end of the book. In all, we have seven appearances: undragoning Eustace, warning those who would do battle at Goldwater/Deathwater Island, appearing to Lucy in the magic book, coming to Lucy after she makes the Dufflepuds visible, as an albatross guiding the *Dawn Treader* out of dangerous waters, speaking to Caspian through the lion's head on his cabin wall, and as a lamb and then a lion appearing to the children from our world, feeding them, and sending them home.

Biblically, seven is the number of perfection, and it is likely that Lewis was deliberate about Aslan's seven appearances in this, the most symbolic of the Narnian *Chronicles*. In Scripture, Jesus is pictured as both lion (ruler) and lamb (sacrifice for sins). He is called the lamb of God. The breakfast of fish on the coals is similar to a breakfast of fish Jesus fixed for His disciples after they had spent the night fishing, soon after He had come back to life (John 21).

Eustace's undragoning apparently takes place in Aslan's country, on a tall mountaintop with a well of living water. Eustace remembered the event like a dream. Up to that point, he had hated the very name Aslan, but now he must submit to Aslan, and he does so willingly.

Navigating Narnia

Dreams and dreamlike states are common in the *Chronicles*. Here are just a few others: in *Wardrobe*, Edmund remembered the lamppost as if in a dream. In *Chair*, Jill dreams of Aslan, who shows her the missed sign, and the Green Witch tries to convince the travelers that Narnia is a dream. Queen Helen in *Nephew* thinks she's dreaming when she is pulled into Narnia.

Aslan himself is made visible by the spell to make the monopods visible. Lucy thinks he is joking when he tells her she has made him visible, but he assures her that he obeys his own rules. He is not "under" the law, but he made the law, and he abides by it. Later Lucy calls to him when the ship seems to be unable to get out of the deep darkness of the frightening land where dreams come true (not longings and dreams, but dreams and nightmares). This passage was heavily revised by Lewis in American editions, to get rid of the sense that he seemed to be trivializing the dreadful dreams when the sailors all laugh at their fear and the island simply disappears. American editions produced after 1994 have returned to the original, unrevised version.

This visit to Narnia will be the last for Edmund and for Lucy. She can hardly bear the thought. Quickly she tells Aslan it is not Narnia so much, but he himself—she can't stand the thought of no longer seeing him. He tells her she can discover him in our world, too, that indeed this is his very reason for taking the children into Narnia, that they might know him here. Any access to his country will come from our world, too. He tells them only that it lies across a river (a biblical metaphor for death) and that he is a Bridge Builder. This is one of the clearest hints in Narnia that Aslan represents Jesus and his country, heaven.

Dufflepuds or Monopods and a Magician

On a well-manicured island, thumping, invisible people have a request—really, a demand: the young girl (Lucy) must go upstairs to the magician's book and conduct a spell for them. In spite of their dubious intent for her, Lucy trusts them and is the first to take them up on their invitation to supper. Her love for creatures who might wish to harm her is as pure as her love for Mr. Tumnus in *Wardrobe*, when he repented his initial desire to kidnap her for the White Witch.

Not till she says the spell can the travelers see what the people look like. Each creature has one big foot on which he hops. The magician, Coriakin, tells Lucy they used to be ordinary dwarfs, but they were conceited and foolish, and he transformed them into Dufflepuds or monopods.

Coriakin feeds Lucy and attempts to give her foods similar to what she would have eaten in her own land. (Lucy makes no comment about whether he succeeds.) Coriakin also sits down with Drinian and magically produces a map of what Drinian has seen on the travels so far. The map is detailed, with magical details so complete that one can look at it with a magnifying glass and see down to the level of individual buildings. (Did Lewis take out a patent on the Internet?) But it shows only what Drinian himself has seen, and, thus, some coastlines and other areas aren't terribly clear.

Ramandu and His Daughter

At the island known as World's End, where Aslan's table is set every evening, the travelers meet a beautiful lady and her father. The father is a retired star, Ramandu. His beautiful daughter will become Caspian's wife and Queen of Narnia. (We are never told her name.) Caspian will pick her up on the voyage returning to Narnia.

Our first glimpse is of great but simple beauty: a door in a hillside opens, and out comes a beautiful girl carrying a tall candle in a silver candlestick. When her father comes out, he does not carry a light because light comes from him. His silver hair and beard both grow to his feet, and his clothing appears to be the wool of silver sheep. He is mild and grave, wise and good.

Ramandu looks much like the hermit Paul in the medieval legend of St. Brendan's voyage to the Land of Promise. Like Ramandu, Paul was for many years fed by an animal.

The Narnians aren't sure whether to trust the strangers. At their table sit three enchanted Narnian lords, apparently in a seven-year sleep. The lady says the lords haven't touched the food, but dare they trust her? They cannot know; they can only choose to believe and to trust. (Reepicheep, naturally, is the first one to dare.) But the table is bountifully filled; we are told that even Cair Paravel never saw a banquet such as this. This is Aslan's table spread plentifully every evening. The banquet is prepared for Aslan's people seeking him, similar to the ultimate banquet in the Bible—the Marriage Supper of the Lamb (Revelation 19:6–9).

In the morning, star father and princess daughter sing up the sun. As they face east, arms upraised, singing, the sun comes up, and from it come thousands of large white birds, singing the same song in wilder tones. One brings the old man a fire-berry from the sun. Much wildness is here, with fear and beauty, though a wildness that is good as Aslan is wild and yet good.

What Should We Watch For?

This book moves fast enough that you can easily miss important elements if you're not careful. Although it is written as various events strung together by voyaging in a ship, it has recurring themes and repeating elements.

Magic—Use and Misuse

Much in this story is magical, good and bad. The most obvious may be the magician's book on the island of the Dufflepuds. The magician uses magic wisely when his charges insist on foolish disobedience that will only make their lives more difficult. They made themselves invisible but have decided that they want to be able to see one another again.

The most magical item we see is the stone knife, the one used by the White Witch to slay Aslan. It is not a common knife, and when one of Narnia's lords grabbed it in anger, all three at the table fell into a seven-year enchanted sleep without dreams.

The magic of the water on Deathwater Island, which turns anything it touches to gold, has killed one of the Narnian lords. It also causes fighting between the *Dawn Treader's* people until Aslan intervenes and erases their memory.

God Sightings

Why would the knife used to kill Aslan be held in honor? It showed Aslan's great love and great power as he rescued Edmund and all of Narnia. Likewise, the cross on which Jesus died is now a powerful symbol of Christianity. By Jesus' death and resurrection, we have life.

Reepicheep's True Courage

Reepicheep is quick to trust others, and he doesn't value his own life. He values honor. Although he is a warrior, when he no longer needs his sword, he tosses it. Courage is the highest of the virtues, according to Lewis in *The Screwtape Letters*—for without courage, chastity or honor or any other virtue succumbs at the first threat to it.

In *Caspian*, our first look at Reepicheep the courageous mouse may have simply seemed foolish. Here we see that his courage sometimes goes beyond wisdom, but it is true courage. He is willing to risk his life for a friend—or for a good adventure.

Eustace's Reformation

Eustace is bad news. He's selfish, whiny, and spoiled, and has no ability to see himself. He needs quite a bit of work on his attitude before he can become a productive member of the company. He is in serious need of a lesson—one he seems unlikely to get. His mother thinks he's perfect, administrators at his school don't believe in any form of discipline, and he won't listen to anyone in Narnia. But then he spends a few days breathing fire and eating raw goats, and he decides the *Dawn Treader* and its crew were a little bit better than he gave them credit for.

He realizes he is a monster cut off from the human race—he has become literally what he had always been figuratively. He's ready to meet Aslan. He has had time to think and to repent. Aslan heals him and forgives him. When Aslan rescues him from his dragon nature and his dragon self, we are told he begins to be a very different boy.

Eustace's main danger isn't the voyage, but his own self-centered little world. Eustace must get to where he relies on another to save him. Self-improvement isn't going to be enough, and he doesn't think he needs improvement. He needs regeneration.

Eustace's first brave act came days later—trying to kill the sea serpent—an act of courage ironically countered by Reep's first statement that they *shouldn't* fight.

God Sightings

Regeneration is the best word for what happened to Eustace. He didn't just change a little bit when he was undragoned; his whole self was renewed and transformed. He had new hopes, dreams, interests, and feelings. Regeneration is what happens when Jesus forgives a person; He gives a whole new life.

The Power of Temptation

Many temptations face the *Dawn Treader* crew and its individual members. We've already looked at some of them, so let's just list them, to be sure you don't miss any:

- As Lucy looks at the book of magic, she experiences the temptation to be really beautiful (which she resists with Aslan's help) and to hear what her friends think of her (to which she succumbs).

- Eustace isn't really even "tempted" in the first half of the book. He simply does or says what he wants, or tries to. The temptation of the riches of the dragon's hoard results in his transformation into a dragon, and his cure.

- The stone knife has proved a temptation to one of the lords, and the lure of the land where dreams come true has trapped another (to his horror, because the island proves to be a land of nightmare-type dreams and not fulfilled desires).

- Deathwater Island is a dangerous temptation to the travelers, and the merpeople could be.

- Caspian's temptation to desert is overcome only by his entire ship's telling him it is inappropriate, and by Aslan himself forbidding it.

In nearly all of these temptations, it takes Aslan (or one of his people) to give the tempted person strength to resist temptation. Scripture tells us that God won't let the Christian be faced with too great a temptation but, like Aslan, will always provide a way to "escape" the temptation (1 Corinthians 10:13).

A Child's-Eye View

This adventurous book has much to whet a child's imagination, especially the child who is drawn to travels and the sea. Its riches include literal treasure, great food, a live dragon, invisible people, and a book of magic spells.

Aslan shows up at unexpected times, in unexpected places, and even in different forms than his lion one.

Children's books can make us less contented with our world or send us back with new admiration—here, we are reminded that our own world is a place of wonder. Caspian is excited to discover Earth is round; Narnian fairy tales have round worlds. It's a good reminder that our own world is every bit as interesting and mysterious as these enchanted islands. (In *Chair*, Caspian tells Aslan he has always wanted to see our world, and he is allowed a brief visit.)

In addition, Aslan tells Lucy plainly that she can know him from our world—a hint for the reader to seek Jesus and come to know Him.

Series-Wide Issues Lewis Develops

Because we see so many Narnian characters in so many different settings, Lewis has a wonderful opportunity to show us what each one is made of and to flesh out many of his typical themes.

Sayings and Sound Advice

After being told she and Edmund can't return to Narnia, Lucy asks Aslan if Eustace can come back—like the apostle Peter asking about John's future when Jesus tells Peter he will have an unpleasant old age (John 21:22). Like Jesus, Aslan pretty much says mind your own business; that's his story, and not yours.

In the use of the stone knife and the magician's book, we have strong suggestions to be careful not to misuse the holy or the magical. Not all magic is good, nor all that is religious; that which has religious power (for good or evil) must be used with care.

Warnings about greed also abound, as we have seen.

Narnian Themes

The power of temptation is vividly demonstrated. Shipmates learn a greater sense of the importance of taking responsibility and trusting others. They also learn to work together and use one another's strengths. Reepicheep is too short to row, but he can stay awake overnight and guard the water supply. Readers learn the importance of reading the right books.

As King Lune tells Shasta in *Horse*, a king cannot please himself with adventures. Much as Caspian wants to journey with Reepicheep to Aslan's country, it is his duty to stay in Narnia and be king.

And finally, in *Voyage* we get one of our clearest statements that the main reason for knowing Aslan in Narnia is to know him here. Although it is not spelled out for us what Aslan means when he tells Lucy this, clearly Lewis meant that knowing Aslan helps us to know Jesus. Loving Aslan helps us see in a fresh new way how lovable—and how good—Jesus is.

Religious References, Mythic Echoes

The mythic elements of this quest journey are numerous, as are the pictures of a Christian life. We won't go into great detail on any of it, but we will let you know what we found out about Lewis's possible sources and ideas for story lines in *Voyage*.

Voyage is the most Arthurian of the *Chronicles*, in some ways reminding us of the Grail quest. *Allusions* are made to both the *Odyssey* (Odysseus and the sirens) and King Arthur (Reepicheep's sword). But *Voyage* more strongly reflects Homer in its story line of voyaging across strange islands.

Narnian Dictionary

An **allusion** is a brief, unexplained hint of a literary or historical character or event. In addition to allusions, Lewis uses borrowings (bringing in characters and events from other sources), echoes or parallels (similar story lines or characters), and influences (more subtle hints of his familiarity with another author, such as word or style choices).

Biblical Parallels

This journey is really about the spiritual life. We see it most clearly in Reepicheep, who is focused on a successful conclusion to the journey and his life. The *Chronicles* mention frequently that Aslan comes from over the sea, and in the end of *Voyage*, Aslan tells Lucy that the way to his country from our world lies across a river. He's referencing the biblical picture of the River Jordan as a symbol for death. (This image was picked up in African American spirituals, John Bunyan's *Pilgrim's Progress*, and many other places.)

The berries like live coals fed to Ramandu every morning are an allusion to Isaiah 6:6–7, where the prophet Isaiah, in a vision, received a coal to cleanse his mouth and make him able to speak for God.

Calling out to Aslan in distress (as Lucy did when the ship was stuck in the land of darkness) is, of course, a reference to the Christian's lifeline of prayer.

Eustace's undragoning is a beautiful image of conversion. He needed to have his old nature removed, yet he was helpless to do it himself. Aslan removed Eustace's old dragonish self, cleansed him, and redressed him. Jesus does the same for each person who comes to Him and says, "Help me. I've tried and tried to make myself better, but I can't do it. I need You to forgive me, clean me up, and make me new."

The lovely story that Lucy read in the magician's book is one she never could remember, but Aslan promised to be telling it to her always. She remembered that it was about a cup, a sword, a tree, and a green hill— elements of religious significance, possibly involving the cup of the Last Supper (Jesus' last meal with His disciples before His death) and His death on a tree on a hill.

Greek

Odysseus and the sirens are, of course, an allusion to a story told in Homer's *Odyssey* (sometimes Odysseus is called Ulysses.) The sirens were singing creatures (usually pictured as women or half-women) who were irresistible to men and who pulled sailors to their deaths.

Odysseus/Ulysses had his men stop up their ears and bind him to the mast so he could not respond to the singing.

Arthurian

When Reepicheep rows to Aslan's country and knows he won't need his sword anymore, he flings it away. It lands upright in the water, like King Arthur's sword. Narnia is very Arthurian, with its pageantry and knights and chivalry, dances and feasts, and much of its speech and manners. Reepicheep is only an exaggeration of the theme, as a miniature medieval knight.

Norse

Pulling into what they would end up calling Dragon Island, voyagers on the *Dawn Treader* found themselves in "a bay encircled by such cliffs and crags that it was like a Norwegian fjord." It seems a good hint that we'll see sights we might not see in England (or America)—including dragons.

A kraken, a sea monster of the sort the voyagers encountered, comes from tales told in Norway and Iceland. Interestingly, the tales seem to be based on a real creature—the giant squid, which has been documented as attacking small ships.

Dropping Hints: Literary Allusions

We've already shown several times when Lewis admits to using a story from another source. In *Voyage*, the whole journey format, many of the stops, and the creatures are borrowed from other writers and pulled into one beautiful tale that is very much Lewis's own.

All Those Other Authors

Monopods were not invented by Lewis, but mentioned in *Natural History* by Pliny the Elder (A.D. 23–79) and in Sir John Mandeville's *Travels* (1371).

Lucy suggests that the dragon (whom none has yet identified as Eustace) is coming to be cured, as in the story of Androcles and the lion. This European fairy tale tells of a lion with a thorn in his front paw, removed by Androcles. The lion later refuses to kill Androcles when they meet in the arena.

Reflections of Lewis's Writings and Life

When Caspian is told that the Lone Island's involvement in the slave trade showed progress and development, he said he'd seen such development in an egg, and there it was rightly called "going bad." Lewis didn't think much of progress as an end in itself; progress is positive only if it is moving toward something good.

Coriakin, ruler of the Dufflepuds, agrees that the Chief Dufflepud isn't very intelligent and isn't really much of a leader to them. But they do not admire or respect Coriakin, and he believes it is better for them to respect their chief than not to respect anybody. Lewis made Narnia a monarchy for the same reason. He believed democracy is probably the healthiest modern form of government, as it keeps the power from all being concentrated into one person, who could easily become corrupt. Still, he believed that people have a natural desire to look up to a ruler, and when they don't have a king, they will instead admire celebrities, which is a far less healthy form of admiration.

The Least You Need to Know

- *Voyage* tells of the most significant event during the life of Caspian X, the voyage to the utter east, to explore uncharted waters and, most important, to find the seven exiled lords.

- The boy Eustace is too focused on his own petty concerns and must be saved from himself.

- Reepicheep desires above all else to reach the end of the world, and Aslan's country, but meanwhile he presses the crew to courage every time they hesitate to taste a new adventure.

Chapter 10

The Silver Chair

In This Chapter

- Eustace's return to Narnia with a schoolmate, Jill Pole
- Aslan's guidance to bring back Prince Rilian before his father's death
- Humans working closely with Narnia's creatures, including owls and a Marsh-wiggle (a *what?*), to follow Aslan's Signs and find Prince Rilian

Prince Rilian has been missing for 10 years, with few clues of his whereabouts—or even whether he is still alive. Many have died searching for him. His father, King Caspian, is aged and worried about his successor. Aslan assigns Jill and Eustace the treacherous task of finding the young Prince, giving them four Signs to help them find the right path and discover where the Prince is.

Through danger and distraction, the most important thing Jill and Eustace can do to find Prince Rilian is to follow the Signs. But that seems the hardest task for them; repeatedly they forget the Signs, mess them up, and even miss seeing them.

As finding the Prince would be impossible without Aslan's Signs, it would probably also be impossible without the aid of an unlikely traveling companion, the gloomy but faithful Puddleglum. Together the three must find the Prince, or perish in the attempt.

Fast Facts

Other titles Lewis considered for this volume were *The Wild Waste Lands*, *Night Under Narnia*, and *Gnomes Under Narnia*. It was dedicated to Nicholas Hardie, son of Inklings member Colin Hardie.

In Narnia, it has been 50 years since *Voyage* (although Eustace estimates 70). With Caspian's assumption to the throne, the castle in use is once again Cair Paravel (although how it was repaired since *Caspian* and how they overcame the handicap of its now being on an island and not a peninsula is never explained). The travelers start in England and end up in Aslan's country, from whence they are sent to the seaside in Narnia and Cair Paravel. The voyage overland takes them to the far North of Narnia, underground beneath Narnia, and finally up into the heart of Narnia—and then back to Aslan's country and home.

For the captive Prince, this is a story of darkness and lies to light and truth; for Jill and Eustace, it is of learning to obey, in spite of continually being distracted by circumstances and by their own desires.

Who Will We Meet?

A good number of this story's cast have been with us before, but all have changed since we last saw them: those who have stayed in Narnia are much older now, and Eustace is not the selfish, whiny brat we met in the early part of *Voyage*. Aslan is still the same lion, but we see him mostly in his own country on this visit.

Voyage ended with Aslan's comment that for those from Earth, the door to his country is from our world. *Chair* begins with children going not directly into Narnia, but through Aslan's country and from there into Narnia. They enter Aslan's country through a literal door, a door in a wall from school.

Jill Pole

Jill Pole attends school at Experiment House with Eustace Scrubb—a school viciously caricatured by Lewis. Jill is a victim of the bullies at school; in our first sight of her, she is hiding from them and crying.

Jill has a few bad habits that can hurt herself and others. Aslan needs to deal with some of these before she is ready for the task he is giving the children. Her tendency to show off hurts Eustace almost immediately, causing him to fall off the cliff and making them mess up the first Sign. Jill wants to justify herself, and as a result, she can't look Aslan in the eye.

Jill at the stream, afraid to approach and afraid not to, is similar to the sinful woman meeting Jesus at the well in John 4. She is face to face with the only one who can forgive her, which is more frightening than it might sound because he is also the one who can condemn her.

The main task of learning the Signs is not to understand the mystery, but to obey. But the children mess up the Signs so thoroughly that Aslan must come to Jill in a dream and show her what she and the others have overlooked. (Repeating signs was a task given to children in *Nephew* also—Polly and Digory must follow signs to find and bring back the magic apple.)

 Navigating Narnia

The Signs by which the travelers will know the Prince:

1. Eustace is to greet an old friend, who can offer aid.
2. They are to travel to the ruined city of the ancient giants.
3. They need to obey the writing on a stone they find there.
4. When asked to do something in Aslan's name, they must do it, for the person who asks is the Prince.

The Signs are really prophecies—Aslan knows in advance what the children will see and what they should do. The ruined giants' city and its writing were there all along, but Aslan's Signs also predicted who Eustace would see first and who would ask a favor in his name.

Missing sleep the first night was enough to make Jill "sick of adventures," although she has a lot more ahead of her. All of Narnia is new to her, and we see it through her eyes—her first view of giants, for instance.

She hasn't had a lot of experience with traveling or dealing with people who may be enemies, so when the Lady of the Green Kirtle (who later proves to be a witch) asks questions, she readily answers.

Eustace Scrubb

We've met Eustace before, in *Voyage*, but he learned his lesson well and is truly a different boy now. He is much better able to be a useful member of the team, although he, like Jill, sometimes fusses and argues and seeks his own best interest ahead of the team's goals.

His first time into Narnia, Eustace spent the whole visit on a sea voyage, and now he spends most of his visit trekking through wilderness—and areas haunted by giants.

At the beginning of *Voyage*, he was mocking his cousins for claims to have been out of the world by magic; in the beginning of *Chair*, he is hesitantly telling a schoolmate about that world. He doesn't know much about Narnia, having never actually been in Narnia proper, but he understands that Aslan isn't someone who can be approached by magic spells.

After meeting the Green Witch, the children fall under the "spell" of their own appetites—they want to believe her and have the chance to indulge themselves after the hardships of traveling. Getting to Harfang becomes the goal of their journey, to the extent that they eventually stop repeating the Signs or talking about Aslan or the lost Prince.

 God Sightings

The *Chronicles* frequently showcase characters tempted by greed or appetite (sin): Edmund's Turkish delight in *Wardrobe*, Deathwater Island in *Voyage*, Digory's temptation by the apple and Uncle Andrew's desires to get rich from the fertility of the young Narnia in *Nephew*, and the temptation here to seek warm beds and good food instead of focusing on Aslan's Signs and the rescue of the Prince.

Aslan

In *Chair*, we see a new side of Aslan that we haven't seen before: the ruler of his own country and the one who gives new life to Caspian, in his country.

Aslan blows the children to Narnia and gives them Signs to find the Prince (which won't look as they expect them to). Later he appears to Caspian on his voyage and tells him to return home because the Prince has been found.

When Aslan speaks to Jill, his voice is "deeper, wilder and stronger" than a man's voice, heavy and golden, and rather frightening. She is afraid but has no choice but to trust him.

At Caspian's funeral procession, when Aslan arrives to send the children home, Jill thinks of all the things she has done wrong: causing Eustace to fall off the cliff, missing three of the Signs, and quarreling. She wants to say she is sorry but can't speak. Aslan understands and forgives her. His presence is enough to lead Jill to repentance, and he understands her repentance without words; once again, Aslan is the "Christ figure" of the story.

Master Glimfeather and Trumpkin

Glimfeather the owl and Trumpkin the dwarf (whom we met in *Caspian*) play somewhat minor roles in this story, but they are important to the beginning of the children's quest. Trumpkin is quite deaf now, and his misunderstandings add humor to the opening pages. He complains that talking animals mumble and mutter now rather than speaking up as they did when he was a young dwarf.

More than 30 people of various species have set out to look for the lost Prince through the years, and none has returned. Caspian will not let anyone else go look for his son, and Trumpkin wouldn't let the children go if he knew of their errand. Glimfeather decides it must be kept a secret. Because Aslan has commanded the quest, it is a lawful one, but wiser for now to keep secret.

Glimfeather isn't overly courageous—he has no desire to travel up north himself—but he helps the children by delivering them to someone who can help them, Puddleglum.

Puddleglum

Puddleglum the *Marsh-wiggle* is so pessimistic that he smokes tobacco with heavy smoke that drifts out of his pipe and down. This might get me stoned by loyal Narnians, but I (Cheryl) didn't like Puddleglum the first time or two that I read this book. He is simply too gloomy. He's not anxious or afraid, but he constantly speaks of what might go wrong. Yet Puddleglum is the best friend the children can have in a dangerous quest.

Narnian Dictionary

What in Narnia is a **Marsh-wiggle?** They resemble frog-men. They are taller than a man but are mostly legs and arms, with webbed hands and feet. They have a muddy complexion and green-gray hair with flat locks like small reeds. They wear earth-colored clothes and live in wigwams in the swamp. They are gloomy and value their privacy, but they have few possessions.

Puddleglum isn't tempted by the hospitality of the giants of Harfang; he is used to hard living and doesn't seek luxury. More important, Aslan didn't mention Harfang in his list of Signs. It cannot be the goal, because Aslan is their guide. Puddleglum's temptation comes in the form of his love for the children in his care. Although he knows better, he gives in and allows them to choose what they desire instead of what is good for them.

Puddleglum is very much the adult in this book, accompanying two young, innocent children whose minds continually wander from their number one priority. It isn't until after Harfang that the children finally consistently trust Puddleglum's leadership.

Puddleglum is loyal to the point of willingly facing death for his friends—and reminding them of Aslan's words when they start forgetting. When the children are despondent from being underground, interestingly, he is the one who offers encouragement. He reminds them that they are back on track and following Aslan's Signs, and thus right where they are supposed to be. When the fourth Sign comes in a way that distresses the children, Puddleglum assures them that they need to obey it anyway, for what is the purpose of memorizing the Signs if they don't obey them?

He alone can overcome the Witch's magic because he is the one who is faithful in his belief in Aslan, regardless of the circumstances.

A Lady in Green and Her Knight

The Green Lady is mysterious; she seems friendly and asks many questions. The Knight with her doesn't say a word. (Is the silent knight a holy knight?)

Later we find out that the Green Lady, by then clearly seen to be a witch, is Queen of Underland. The Knight and the earthmen all come under her command. There doesn't seem to be any real connection between the Green Witch and the White Witch of *Wardrobe* (who is also Jadis from Charn, in *Nephew*). But they are both northern witches, and they have much the same purpose—power at any cost.

At the castle in Underland, the travelers are happy to hear the voice of a human at the top of the stairs. They discover that the young man is the silent knight who accompanied the Lady of the Green Kirtle a few days earlier. Now he speaks—but he speaks mostly of the great virtues of the Lady.

Although usually only the Queen (the Green Witch) stays with the Knight during his daily hour of frightful enchantment, today she is away, and he pleads with the travelers to stay so that he will not be alone. He tells them that he turns into a snake during his enchantment, and thus he is carefully bound to a silver chair—bound at ankles, knees, waist, elbows, and wrists. (Of course, we've never met a snake that has ankles, knees, a waist, elbows, or wrists. We think we might be afraid he'd slither out.)

When the Witch returns and finds the visitors from Overland, she is enraged and seeks to captivate them. She lulls their reasoning powers to sleep. Her spells make it hard even to think straight. This is a key part of the book, as *Chair* has much to show about how one's thinking affects one's actions. The travelers must continue to believe in Aslan even in the gloom and magic or they are lost—as the Knight himself was, when he surrendered to the Witch's magic long ago.

Giants of Harfang

Rarely do we meet gentle giants in literature, although some giants have fought on Aslan's side in various battles (most notably, Rumblebuffin in *Wardrobe*). The Lady of the Green Kirtle has assured the travelers that Harfang is home to gentle giants and that they will gladly include the travelers in their autumn feast. Indeed, the giants go out of their way to be sure they have good accommodations and plentiful food, as the Lady told them. She may not have told them *everything* they need to know, but she never actually lied to them, either.

The children and the Marsh-wiggle decide they don't want to be part of the feast, after all, once they realize they have missed another of Aslan's Signs in their eagerness for good beds and warm food. (A look at the giants' cookbook also proves quite unappetizing.)

The giants are a sentimental folk, and their womenfolk cry just looking at the sweet little children. Jill takes advantage of that sentimentality in a wonderful, wise plan to get the travelers out of the castle and back following the Signs, convincingly acting like an inquisitive little girl so she can ask questions that will help them escape.

The giant bridge and ancient road should be indications they are nearing the ancient ruined city they're seeking. But soon they are traveling through a blinding snowstorm. Lewis doesn't mention it, but we suspect the snow just might be brought about by the Green Witch, if she has any of the same powers as the White Witch in *Wardrobe*.

Earthmen in Underland

The earthmen, really goblins or gnomes, are a diverse bunch of various heights and appearances. But they have a few things in common: all are pale, all carry three-pronged spears, and all look very, very sad.

They are so sad that Puddleglum believes they might help him learn to be more serious. Together they seem a dismal group of jailers to the travelers. *Chair*'s earthmen bear a marked similarity to the goblins in MacDonald's *Phantastes*. MacDonald also uses goblins in *The Princess and the Goblin*.

Magic and Myth

The travelers meet two other types of beings in Underland, setting the stage for *Battle*. Father Time and multiple dragons and lizardlike beings sleep in the underground cave, waiting to awaken at the end of time. Watch for them to appear again at the end of *Battle*.

After the Witch is killed, the travelers find to their surprise that the earthmen have been slaves, kept by the Witch against their will. Their real home is deeper in the earth, in a land known as Bism. They celebrate their freedom to return, setting off fireworks and turning handstands. Their gloom was not part of their personality after all, but a result of their slavery and being forced to live higher than they prefer.

Prince Rilian

Ten years before this story began, Rilian's mother died, bitten by a serpent. Rilian sought her killer to slay it and ended up obsessed with the Lady he met in the glade where his mother died. One day he disappeared. His father, Caspian, is now near death, and Aslan has sent the children to find Rilian and return him home in time to secure his throne.

When we finally meet Prince Rilian, he may not be exactly what we expect. He is under a spell, and in that spell he longs to be King of Narnia by force—much like Edmund was willing to rule Narnia as a usurper, when the throne was really his by right. The travelers rescue him, and he is heartily glad to be returning to Narnia as its legal Prince.

When the travelers dig out from Underland with Rilian, Narnians know him immediately, although he has been gone for 10 years and some of them have never seen him. He has the look of a true King of Narnia. This isn't the first time a Narnian is identified by his "look."

In *Wardrobe*, for instance, Mr. Beaver says that Edmund has the look of someone who has been with the Witch and eaten her food. Lewis might have agreed with Lincoln that "every man over 40 is responsible for his face"—that is, that our faces show something of our life choices, good or bad.

What Should We Watch For?

Most of the troubles in this book come about because Jill and Eustace aren't paying attention. So we suggest that as you read, you do pay attention. You wouldn't want to be deceived by any wicked people who pretend to be nice, or to assume bad motives of people who are really your friends. Here are some specific things that are worth noting.

The Importance of the Signs

Finding the Prince may not be all that difficult if the children follow the Signs. Jill accidentally gets separated from Eustace just when they should both be hearing the Signs together, and Eustace misses hearing the first Sign. Had he heard it in time, this story might have been very different, as they would have probably had assistance from Narnia's king on their quest. Now they must travel the wild wastelands on foot. The other three Signs are equally important. But it proves far too easy to get distracted from them.

Even when the travelers are back on track and headed for the fourth Sign, the children and Puddleglum are in a boat on a river in Underland for such a long time that they begin to wonder if they have dreamed of blue sky and sun. The stage is set for them to doubt the reality they know to be true, when confronted with an insistently false reality.

Following the Signs is akin to memorizing and obeying Scripture. Sometimes it's hard to do the right thing, but knowing the right thing ahead of time, before temptation comes, and resolving to obey no matter what is half the battle. The Bible even tells us that obedience is better than all sorts of good things offered after disobedience to "make up for" our error: "To obey is better than sacrifice" (1 Samuel 15:22).

Whether Appearances Are Really What They Seem

Much in this story is not what it first seems, including the Signs themselves. Puddleglum himself is not, nor are the silent Knight, the giants of Harfang, or the earthmen. Read between the lines—and look for other surprises.

Doing What Must Be Done

Aslan's directions are clear. He hasn't presented a multiple-choice test or a road map with some possible routes marked out with question marks. Puddleglum consistently does what he should do (although, in the case of going to Harfang, he probably wasn't insistent enough). But the children waver. Sometimes they do what they are supposed to; sometimes they do what they want to. They are at their best when they put one foot in front of the other, resolutely doing what they have to do and knowing that Aslan will bring it all together somehow.

The Witch, by means of a green powder that produces a sweet and pacifying smell, begins to convince them that their memories are all a dream. There has never been any world but hers. Puddleglum recovers himself enough to stamp out much of the Witch's fire and to tell her that he and his friends will leave to seek Narnia, even if she's right and it doesn't exist. We are told that the fire hurt Puddleglum less than it would have hurt the others, but clearly he was sacrificing for the good of his friends.

The Nature of Deceit

What is false comes in many guises in this story: magic that undermines the senses (the Witch's green powder and smooth words), magic that overpowers one's own choices, a snowstorm that hides reality, words that are true but intended to deceive (like the children's invitation to be part of the giants' autumn feast), and the various enchantments in Underland.

It is good that the children and Puddleglum have something definite and unambiguous to guide them—Aslan's Signs. Although the Signs are not always what they expect to see, they are clear when they appear.

The Witch works by captivating minds, encouraging fuzzy thinking and false logic. She mocks the country up above *without* disproving it, much as many attacks on Christianity are done. (Lewis was giving a good solid example of relativistic thinking.) She works not by logic, but by sheer repetition; she's a "naturalist" who denies and mocks the possibility of the supernatural rather than attempting to disprove it.

True Loyalty to Truth

The children want to find Prince Rilian, and they want to follow Aslan. But Puddleglum is the one who is *determined* to follow Aslan. The travelers' individual understanding of truth, and of Narnia, is pictured well in the scene where they realize they have been eating a talking stag. Puddleglum, a loyal Narnian, is deeply sickened, like finding he'd eaten a baby. Eustace is distressed because he has been in Narnia before and he understands it is taboo—but he doesn't feel it as deeply as Puddleglum does. Jill's reaction is more like that of somebody who doesn't want to eat a rabbit or deer because they're cute—she is unhappy about it but doesn't feel deeply that it is morally wrong. (Later she comes to a greater understanding.)

A Child's-Eye View

Upon entering Narnia, we experience vivid sights and sounds through Jill's senses: the bright colors of the crowd, the sounds of the sea, and Jill's shock at seeing that only about a fifth of the crowd is human.

Chair has much to appeal to the imagination of an adventurous child, including two different varieties of living giants *and* a ruined giant city and bridge. The description of the giants includes what they look like, a game, their quarreling, and even giant home life and a hunting party setting out from Harfang.

We also come face to face with a witch and a knight. Jill and Eustace travel on owls. At the end, the children experience an unheard-of privilege—riding on centaurs to go meet King Caspian. We have the great picture of real gold and diamonds in Bism, growing and alive, rather than dead like our metals and gemstones.

Aslan is fearsome, yet the host in his own world, a new way of seeing him. The children interact with him directly, and he sends them to Narnia on his breath. He even deals with the bullies who have been pestering them, because their teachers won't.

Narnia is alive and wild (and not at war); we even get to see it on the occasion of a yearly festival, the great snow dance. And finally, this book has much humor and begs a child to feel affection for the aged and half-deaf dwarf Trumpkin—and the ever-gloomy Puddleglum.

Series-Wide Issues Lewis Develops

Chair literally covers new ground from the other books in the series, moving much farther North and also having much of the traveling take place underground. Puddleglum is a whole new sort of creature, too. But new characters and new places serve only to enhance the Narnian themes of learning to love Aslan, taking responsibility, and learning to work together virtuously.

Sayings and Sound Advice

In Underland, the oft-repeated saying is "Many fall down, but few return to the sunlit lands." The theme could be rather discouraging to the Narnians, except that they are in Aslan's paws and he has led them here.

Inviting a centaur for a weekend is a very serious thing; be sure you have enough food for the man stomach and the horse stomach—and the time it takes for him to eat breakfast. You'll probably never need to know that, but the respect the children learned for centaurs may come in handy if you are a host or a guest of people from a vastly different background from your own.

Narnian Themes

Puddleglum states the thesis very concisely in the exact middle of the book: "Aslan's instructions always work: there are no exceptions."

Today many people who say they are Christians will also say that obedience to the Bible is too difficult. We really "can't" be expected to obey the harder commands that go against our own desires and our culture. But Puddleglum reminds us that it's not our job to see how everything comes together; it's our job to obey.

Later Puddleglum says there are no accidents when one's guide is Aslan. Puddleglum is not at all confident about circumstances, but he is supremely confident in Aslan.

Religious References, Mythic Echoes

Chair is an archetypal journey into the underworld (often seen as Hell, the Realm of the Dead, or Hades) to bring back a captive. Orpheus, for example, tries to rescue his wife, Eurydice, from Hades but fails because he turns and looks at her. In one of the most debated passages in Scripture, there is a suggestion of Christ's descent into Hell in the period between His death and His resurrection, to bring out captives (Ephesians 4:7–10).

Rilian's speech not to free him is like Odysseus's command to his crew, to keep him bound no matter what he says, lest he seek the sirens.

Biblical Parallels

The idea of a serpent tempter is first seen in Genesis 3, when Satan comes to Eve in the form of a talking serpent. A serpent probably wasn't seen as bad at that point. Satan probably ruined the reputation of all good snakes everywhere.

Jill on the mountaintop getting the Signs is reminiscent of Moses on the mountaintop receiving the Ten Commandments (see Exodus 19).

Jill tells Aslan that they called to him, and he sets her straight about who initiated contact: "You would not have called to me unless I had been calling to you." That is a suggestion of God's electing, or choosing and then calling, the believer for salvation, as presented in Romans 8:28–30.

Aslan weeping over Caspian before bringing him back to life is similar to Jesus weeping over Lazarus in John 11 and then restoring him.

First John 1:7 and 2:3 tell us that we can say we know Jesus only if we keep His commandments. That doesn't mean perfection, but we can't claim to love Jesus if we don't even care what He says.

Aslan also readily forgave Jill's failings at the end. As the Bible says about the Lord, "He knows our frame; He remembers that we are dust" (Psalm 103:14). The reference to people being dust reminds us of the creation story, when Adam was made out of the ground. That doesn't mean that sin is okay. But it does mean that He understands our weaknesses, and He forgives us when we ask Him to.

Greek

Centaurs appear in many Greek myths, as well as in much art and literature, such as the *Iliad*. (The centaurs in Narnia seem to be patterned after Cheiron, or Chiron, in the *Iliad*.) The Greek poet Pindar was the first person to describe them as half-man, half-horse.

Eustace and Jill being blown off the cliff to Narnia is rather like Zephyrus carrying Psyche in the old version of "Cupid/Eros and Psyche."

Werewolves also appear in Greek myths and in those of many other cultures, although their specific attributes vary.

The Green Witch is like Lamia from Greek mythology—part woman, part serpent. Spenser's *Faerie Queene* has such a creature as well—the enchantress Error, who becomes a serpent and tries to wind around the Red Cross Knight. So does Lewis's friend Charles Williams in his *Place of the Lion*.

Arthurian

Young readers might not understand the full mythic importance of the Lady of the Green Kirtle in *Chair*, but if they later read the medieval poem *Sir Gawain and the Green Knight*, they will find the same lady there.

Norse

Stories about giants are found in literature of many lands, including European, Norse, and Greek. Giants are a significant part of *Chair*, with three different cultures represented: living giants out in the wilderness playing a game, a ruined city of giants with a great bridge leading to it, and the giants of Harfang (who could be the descendants of the giants from the ruined city).

Dropping Hints: Literary Allusions

Lewis used quite a few different stories as background to *Chair*.

All Those Other Authors

Underland is like Plato's cave, whose inhabitants mistake shadows for reality, as the Witch tries to have her captives do.

The Knight, when met underground, is said to be dressed all in black and looking rather like Hamlet, an obvious allusion to Shakespeare's *Hamlet*.

Reflections of Lewis's Writings and Life

Puddleglum was based on Lewis's gardener, the ever-pessimistic but always loyal Fred Paxford. Both the man and the Marsh-wiggle specialize in gloomy predictions but loyal friendship.

In addition, long hikes with friends were among Lewis's greatest pleasures. Although we're fairly sure that giants had died out in England by his day, he probably based this journey on some of his own.

The Least You Need to Know

- The most important task given to Eustace and Jill is to follow Aslan's Signs and rescue young Prince Rilian.

- Puddleglum the Marsh-wiggle seems to be a discouraging traveling companion, but he keeps the children on track, reminds them of the Signs, and saves their lives—all because of his steadiness and his loyalty to Aslan.

- Aslan is fully in charge, bringing children in from our land and predicting the future in the form of four Signs.

The Horse and His Boy

In This Chapter

- The lands beyond Narnia and Aslan's presence beyond Narnia

- Two horses and their riders—all with their own reasons for choosing to travel toward Narnia and freedom

- A story that takes place during the reign of the Pevensies and is told thereafter

If a gallop across the desert on a well-trained war horse—a *talking* war horse—appeals to you, then perhaps you will find yourself envying Shasta in *Horse*. Not so fast. The horse, Bree, is in charge of Shasta's ride. And a girl, Aravis, on another horse is tolerating Shasta's presence only because she likes talking to Bree. This might be a long ride.

The Horse and His Boy is a tale of life in the time of Narnia's Golden Age (the rule of the Pevensies), but it shows us very little of life within Narnia. Mostly we see Narnia's neighboring lands, Calormen, a long-time enemy looking for a chance to destroy Narnia (a chance that comes in *Battle*), and Archenland, a tiny neighboring country that is a close ally of Narnia. Many Archenland kings are descended from King Frank, the first king of Narnia.

Fast Facts

A clear theme of *The Horse and His Boy* is slavery to freedom. Even Aravis is not free; she is under the burden of the expectations that come with her rank, which includes marrying someone she despises. The children and horses have much to learn about freedom, including its responsibilities and the way other free people must be treated. But probably the greatest theme of *Horse* is providence, the way God—or, in this case, Aslan—works behind the scenes of our lives.

God Sightings

Providence is God's care and protection, including common, daily provision, such as the rain to grow our food. In *Horse,* Aslan works directly, making sure that certain events come together to keep a person or a country safe. Romans 8:28 in the New Testament, which says that God works all things together for His children's good, is the most famous statement about providence.

Voyage, Horse, and *Chair* were all written in 1950; *Horse* was published in 1954. Originally, it was published near the last (number five of seven), but chronologically it is third, because the story takes place during the fifteenth year of the reign of the Pevensie children.

Horse is the only book in the *Chronicles* that does not have any new children entering Narnia from our world. The Pevensies are already there, young adults now, established as kings and queens. In fact, Susan comes dangerously close to getting married; the man who is courting her is a scoundrel, so it is a very good thing she doesn't.

Who Will We Meet?

In *Horse*, we see some of the philosophies of Narnia's greatest enemy, Calormen, and we get a chance to compare life perspectives, or worldviews, among the three countries of Narnia, Archenland, and Calormen. But we also read a story of an event that is told in Narnia long afterward—an event in which Aslan worked to bring two children and two talking horses to Archenland and Narnia, and allowed them to save both countries from destruction.

Until the middle of this book, we have a whole new cast of characters— most of them from Calormen and Archenland, not from Narnia.

Shasta and Arsheesh

Arsheesh is a poor fisherman, and his boy, Shasta, is little more than his slave when the story begins. Arsheesh doesn't have much part in the story, but Shasta is one of its main characters. Shasta is young and limited in his view of the world. Because men from his village always go south, he finds the South uninteresting and yearns for the mysterious North. One thinks of Lewis as a child, bored by the practical political discussions of men who talked with his father, but enchanted by make-believe and tales of other times and places.

Shasta has never learned it is wrong to listen behind doors, rather conveniently for us, because the information he learns by eavesdropping is quite useful on at least two occasions. When he discovers Arsheesh is not his father, it gives him hope—but hope only for a good master, not for freedom. When Bree, the talking horse, tells him his master (who wants to buy Shasta) is hard on slaves, Shasta considers running away—a happy choice for Bree, because he, too, wants to run away but can't do so without a person. This is a new twist on the classical story of a man existing only among animals (*Tarzan of the Apes*) or a boy and a horse (*The Black Stallion*) in that, in this case, the horse is the one who helps the pair to survive.

Shasta begins the story as an ignorant boy, and he has much to learn throughout the story. But he willingly learns from all he meets, from

Bree to Aravis, from the Hermit to Aslan and King Lune. His humility and teachability prepare him for a greater role than that of slave boy.

Breehy-hinny-brinny-hoohy-hah (Call Him Bree)

Obviously, the name by which Bree introduces himself to Shasta is his own horse name, not that given to him by his Tarkaan master. His name is the sound of a horse's whinny. (The same is true of the second horse, Hwin, also. The mice Reepicheep and Peepiceek, in *Voyage*, are also named for the sounds they make.)

Bree takes the lead from the beginning, insisting that Shasta may not use reins or spurs, and that he himself will choose directions. Until they pass through the city of Tashbaan, he is the best leader. Right away, he's wise enough to leave hoof prints in the direction his Tarkaan would suspect he would go. His Tarkaan doesn't know he's a talking horse, or smarter than any ordinary horse. But once he gets beyond territory he knows, his leadership isn't as wise or as skilled.

Bree loves rolling but isn't sure Narnian horses roll. He's overly concerned about this trivial point of etiquette and vain about his good looks and long tail. Bree's self-conceit is keeping him from Narnia. It isn't enough for him to learn that he isn't as great as he thinks he is, because that hurts his pride but doesn't yet teach him humility. Even meeting Aslan doesn't turn him away from his concern with himself, and we don't know if he ever really learns this lesson.

As they prepare to enter Narnia, Bree's nervousness and self-consciousness turns to gloom. We aren't really sure whether he ever learns complete self-forgetfulness or enjoys Narnia. All along, his desire for Narnia has been mostly nostalgia from his colthood rather than a real awareness of what Narnia is like. Although his cry is "Narnia and the North!" that becomes a habit.

Aravis and Hwin

Bree and Shasta aren't the only pair seeking Narnia and the North. Along the way, a lion (hmm, any guesses as to *which* lion?) forces the pair to link up with a girl, Aravis, and a talking mare, Hwin, who are also traveling to Narnia. Aravis is a young, proud Tarkheena fleeing an undesirable arranged marriage.

Bree and Aravis do most of the talking after the two parties join forces because they have a lot in common in rank and interests. Aravis wants freedom for herself, but she still expects the old hierarchies—she treats Shasta as her slave, Hwin as "her" horse. (Hwin is no longer Aravis's horse, but a free Narnian.) It is very hard for Aravis, as well as for Bree, to travel through Tashbaan in disguise. They are used to having status and looking their best.

Narnian Dictionary

The *Tisroc* was the ruler of Calormen, similar to a pharaoh, and was believed to be descended from the god Tash. *Tarkaans*, lords, were descendants of the Tisroc, and *Tarkheenas* were their wives or daughters. A *vizier* was a high ranking adviser, and the grand vizier held the Imperial seal.

Bree swears "by the Lion" or "by the Lion's mane," although we learn later that he doesn't really believe in the Lion; Aravis swears as a Calormene, "by Tash," and we never learn whether she believes in Tash.

Throughout the book, we see frictions between the humans who are traveling together. They come from very different backgrounds, and they don't like, respect, or understand each other very well at first.

Hwin is the first of the party to approach Aslan when they meet him in Archenland because she is the least encumbered by herself. (Shasta is not with them at the time, but he has already met Aslan.)

Magic and Myth

Are talking horses an odd mount? Children who visit Narnia from our land never seem to ride a horse (even a talking horse). Susan and Lucy have at least two rides on Aslan, in *Wardrobe* and *Caspian*, and Digory rides on a flying horse, Fledge, in *Nephew*. In *Chair*, Jill and Eustace ride on owls and centaurs and—the oddest ride of all—Aslan's breath.

Royalty

In *Horse*, we see royalty from three countries: Narnia, its ally Archenland, and the enemy country of Calormen. It's a good chance to compare and contrast the nations, their cultures, and their worldviews.

Corin, Archenland's prince, is traveling in Calormen with the Narnian royal entourage as a friend of Queen Susan. King Edmund is also with the party, as is Tumnus the faun.

The Narnians have come to Calormen because Prince Rabadash, the eldest son of the Tisroc, has proposed marriage to Susan. They have decided he is a completely unsuitable match for her, and now the Narnians will have to be superbly careful about how to get out of Calormen without being killed or taken as prisoners if Susan refuses her rabidly rash suitor. (Get it, Rabadash?)

The city of Tashbaan has crowded, noisy, smelly streets. Its only traffic rule is that the less important yield the right of way to the more important. Lords and ladies are carried on litters through the city streets by slaves. The city has plenty of statues of its gods and heroes—but these show impressive peoples, not pleasant ones.

Calormen is based mostly on the ancient Persian and Turkish empires; Calormenes are modeled after Arabs in *A Thousand and One Nights*, which was written by Middle Easterners, and Middle Eastern folklore.

When the Narnian nobility come through town, they are in stark contrast: they are walking, dressed in colorful clothes, carrying straight swords rather than the curved Calormene scimitars. They are not grave and mysterious, but approachable—chatting and laughing. One is even whistling. Calormen is a country of strict, even grim hierarchy; Narnia is a land where nobles do not see themselves as better than their countrymen and where they can therefore relax and experience life's joys and social pleasures.

In a moment of carelessness, Shasta is seized, mistaken for Corin. His behavior puzzles the Narnians. His upbringing has been quite different from Corin's; he doesn't act noble, and he doesn't admit the fault they believe he has committed. He doesn't dare tell them the truth because he doesn't know that noble people will treat him kindly. Corin himself is adventurous and eager to fight in the battle, and he finds Shasta's story truly adventurous. Corin needs to learn more responsibility, and Shasta needs to learn better manners, but in Aslan's good time, both are learning what they need to know.

Lasalareen

Lasalareen plays a relatively minor role in the story, mostly a comic one, but she shows us the kind of life that Aravis is fleeing. Lasalareen is Aravis's friend, and the time spent in her house gives Aravis some very necessary information. But it also shows Aravis the reasons she simply must make it safely to Narnia.

Lasalareen is vain, self-centered, and helpless, interested only in clothes and parties and connections with important people. Aravis needs her help to escape the city, and Lasalareen gives it, but quite unwillingly; she is far too concerned about her own trivial pursuits even to empathize with Aravis's urgency or her desire to avoid this marriage. The meal she serves Aravis is mostly sweets.

Aravis is polite as she leaves, thanking her hostess and giving her blessing. But she is honest, too. Lasalareen has a "lovely life" ... but it wouldn't suit her. Aravis is more interested in outdoor activities and finds the palace politics tedious.

Lewis has been accused of being a chauvinist in his portrayal of girl characters. But here we clearly see that Lasalareen is limited to a decorative but useless function, and the more skilled Aravis is better prepared for life and even for the role of a princess. Elsewhere, Lucy's femininity doesn't keep her from braving the dread magician in *Voyage*, and Jill Pole in *Battle* is the best navigator in Narnia's woods, though she is the only female in the group of three people.

Lasalareen's silliness helps Aravis begin to appreciate traveling with Shasta, and she tells Lasalareen with no regrets that she, too, will be a nobody in Narnia. As it turns out, she will be a princess in Archenland instead, but she won't be the air-headed, vain princess that she was reared to be.

King Lune

King Lune rules Archenland, Narnia's ally, justly and wisely. We met one of his sons, Corin, traveling in Tashbaan with Queen Susan, King Edmund, and Tumnus the faun.

King Lune is jolly, fat, and apple-cheeked, with twinkling eyes. He is friendly and welcoming, and has integrity—exactly the man you might choose to have as a father if you found out the man who had raised you was not really your father.

King Lune talks to the horses and asks them questions about their families and the areas of Narnia where they grew up. It is their first time talking to an adult human as an equal, and they are shy, but King Lune has spent his life in Archenland; he is used to talking with animals, and he doesn't hold himself aloof from his subjects.

Navigating Narnia

As soon as the travelers enter Archenland, they meet a 109-year-old hermit who watches current events unfold in a pool of water. He doesn't know the future, but the present. He is able to provide aid and comfort for the weary ones—except for Shasta, whom he encourages to hurry to Anvard in time to warn King Lune about Rabadash's approach.

Aslan

Aslan shows up repeatedly during this story, but because he is appearing to people and horses who do not yet know him, his identity isn't revealed until near the end. Then we find out he has been working behind the scenes the whole time, and showing himself periodically as well.

After Shasta delivers the message of enemies from Calormen to King Lune, he soon finds himself alone, hungry, and tired, in a strange country.

Soon Shasta has a strange companion. He realizes that a large animal has been walking beside him for some time, so he asks who is there. A voice from the darkness says "Myself" three times, in different tones.

Shasta tells his sorrow to the being, who ends up being Aslan. Aslan breathes on him to prove he isn't a ghost. As morning comes and he sees Aslan, he falls on his face before him, with no words. He quickly and easily submits to Aslan, showing his own wisdom and humility.

Aslan's three statements of "Myself" and his listening to Shasta's troubles are a reminder of the Old Testament story from 1 Kings 19:11–12. Elijah is standing on a mountain, watching for God's presence. He sees a great strong wind, an earthquake, and a fire—but God is not in any of these manifestations. And then the quiet, still voice of God calls Elijah's name, asks what is troubling him, and then God listens.

Meanwhile, Aslan soon appears to the other travelers, who are staying with the hermit. Hwin willingly approaches him, and he explains his part in the story of their travels—but only the part that concerns each of them, because he never tells someone anyone else's story.

God Sightings

When Shasta asks the being walking beside him in the darkness who he is, Aslan says "Myself" three times—once low and deep, once loud and cheerful, and once in a very soft whisper. Lewis says in a letter that this is a hint of the Trinity—God in the form of three persons: Father, Son, and Holy Spirit.

What Should We Watch For?

Even readers who are quite familiar with Narnia will find themselves in unfamiliar territory here, traveling through other lands. You'll get the most out of the book if you know a few things to look for.

The Ever-Changing Truth of Shasta's Identity

Shasta begins the story as the apparent son and virtual slave of a fisherman. As he takes on a new identity as a traveler, he finds out more and more of his background. Aslan has even played a role in it long before this story started, many years ago.

Shasta has a lot to learn about being free. When he first meets the Narnians, it simply doesn't occur to him to ask for their help or to tell them the truth (the truth as far as he knows it, which isn't much—but he knows he isn't Prince Corin, as they think he is, and he chooses not to tell them that). He's used to having plans interrupted by adults. He doesn't know how noble, free people act. When he hesitantly suggests to Corin (the real Corin) that Corin might tell the others the truth, Corin is indignant—telling the truth is the obvious thing to do, and the only option.

> **Navigating Narnia**
>
> *Horse* was dedicated to David and Douglas Gresham. Lewis dedicated all the *Chronicles* to children of his friends (except *Battle*, which has no dedication), but he probably never guessed that he was dedicating this book to children who would be his future stepsons when he married their mother, Joy Davidman Gresham.

Truth and Fiction About Narnia ... and Aslan

Bree says Aslan isn't really a lion, but even the Calormenes speak of him as a lion. Bree is speaking from ignorance, not knowledge, but doesn't know it until he meets Aslan. The Calormenes, however, think of Aslan as a lion-shaped demon.

The hundred years of winter in Narnia have only recently come to an end. While the White Witch ruled, Narnia wasn't a desirable country. (We presume that Calormen wasn't strong enough to try to invade *before* the Witch's rule.) Now a vibrant, free country is an offense to Calormen, which would love the opportunity to invade it.

Learning to Work Together

Bree has a hard time accepting Shasta as anything but an ignorant boy traveling with him. Bree and Aravis both consider themselves superior to their traveling partners. But all need to work together. Shy Hwin proves to be the one who is most determined to run her fastest and beat Rabadash's army to Anvard, and ignorant Shasta is brave enough to face a lion as he would a stray dog. All the teammates must learn what it means to be free, and the lowliest members of the party are probably the closest ones to that knowledge.

Romans 12:3–5 is an important passage that could have been beneficial to Aravis and Shasta. It deals with the need for humility and for members of a body to work together in unity for the good of the whole body.

A Child's-Eye View

Talking horses, charging lions, princes and kings and queens … and a long journey with no adults to give directions, but only two children and two horses.

For boys (and girls) who love adventure stories, and girls (and boys) who love horse stories, *Horse* offers a page-turning, suspenseful tale … a story that almost could have taken place in our world, if it weren't for those talking horses (and that lion).

Here we receive hints of a story that is never fully told, a lay of "Fair Olvin and Giant Pire." Mount Pire is the mountain seen off in the distance as the travelers make their way to Anvard, and the story says that it used to be a living two-headed giant. Lewis could perhaps have developed a book about that tale, as he wrote this book about the tale of two horses and two children traveling across the desert. Child readers will have to imagine the details on their own.

Series-Wide Issues Lewis Develops

Once again, characters must learn to get past their own selfishness, learn the value of others, and work together. They also must learn what it means to be free—and willing servants of Aslan.

Rabadash, the eldest son of the Tisroc, chooses to attack Archenland and Narnia in a time of peace, the act of a traitor (and a spurned suitor). Those he has attacked offer him mercy, which he scorns. They provide him good food and a fine room while they figure out what to do with him, but he refuses to eat or sleep, instead stamping and cursing. Aslan also offers mercy. But mercy soon turns into justice, as the fool becomes an ass, known in the future to his own people as Rabadash the Ridiculous.

Sayings and Sound Advice

A Calormene saying is used by several characters: a person says he was sad with the phrase "the sun was darkened in my eyes."

The narrator tells us that people with similar experiences and interests can hardly help talking about them, and if you are present, you might at times feel left out. It's a handy thing for children to learn, lest they feel needless offense.

It's convenient for a story to have characters overhear others' plans—this tale wouldn't have happened without Shasta overhearing the Tarkaan talking with Arsheesh and overhearing the Narnians making their plans, and Aravis overhearing Rabadash planning to overthrow Archenland and Narnia. But readers are reminded, along with Shasta, that one who doesn't wish to be thought a traitor should try not to hear plans meant for others' ears.

King Lune instructs his son never to taunt a man except when he is stronger than you; taunting one who is weaker is mere bullying. He also instructs his son and heir that a king's duty is primary: a king is as tied to his crown as a sentry is to his post, whether he likes it or not. Caspian's subjects reminded him of this truth when he wanted to desert at the end of *Voyage* and sail for Aslan's country instead of returning home; a king has no choice about his kingship.

Narnian Themes

Those who desire freedom must learn what freedom really means. From the beginning of the story, Bree refuses to say "the Tisroc—may he live forever." He is a free Narnian, and that's slaves' talk. And yet he isn't quite as ready for freedom as he thinks, and neither are the others.

Religious References, Mythic Echoes

Readers have sometimes thought Lewis was caricaturing Muslims with his Calormenes. But Islam is monotheistic (believing in only one deity), and there are several gods in Calormen. Tash is actually an

Efreet (a demon with a hideous appearance and foul odor). But not all of Lewis's depictions of the Calormenes are negative. Aravis and Emeth are both Calormenes, and Aslan's country has a replica of Tashbaan in *Battle.* The Tisroc in Calormen finally finds his origin in Nisroch, a Babylonian god mentioned in 2 Kings 19:37.

Calormenes thought of Narnia as inhabited by demons, especially a lion-shaped one. Yet as we see in *Battle,* the Calormenes' primary god, Tash, really is a demon. (They call him "Tash the irresistible, the inexorable," but *irresistible* here surely must not mean desirable!) The grand vizier complains that Narnian poetry is not "useful," but is all about love and war. Calormen is a very *practical* country, but not a beautiful one. Perhaps its only beauty is its people's storytelling ability and the fine clothing of its upper classes.

Biblical Parallels

Aslan's working behind the scenes to bring together events both important and seemingly insignificant is a good illustration of God's providence, or working in lives of individuals and nations.

We see grace offered to Rabadash and refused because of his pride. We see the error and danger of pride and the need of Bree and Aravis to humble themselves to be ready to receive greater blessings than they can when pride is in the way.

The idea of a "scapegoat" has made it into our cultural lexicon, but it was originally a Hebrew practice from the Old Testament, specifically Leviticus 16. Once a year, on the Day of Atonement, two goats were selected. The sins of the Israelites were symbolically placed on the goats. One was then killed as a sin offering. The sins of the people were confessed over the second one, which was sent into the wilderness as a scapegoat.

Arthurian

The radiance and sweet fragrance of Aslan (particularly his mane) was based on descriptions of the Holy Grail, according to Lewis's brother.

Norse

The image of the mysterious, almost mythical North is prevalent throughout this book. The repeating vision is for "Narnia and the North." That mystery in our world might be best exemplified by the otherworldly, haunting myths of the Nordic races.

Dropping Hints: Literary Allusions

Horse is an extended tale—an event that could be summarized in two or three sentences is drawn out into its full detailed plot. The story is fully realized by Lewis but isn't original to him at all.

All Those Other Authors

Horse was heavily influenced by *Arabian Nights*, which Lewis didn't like. In fact, his characters are *fleeing* Calormen. They are seeking Aslan instead of their false gods. *Horse* actually presents a milder version of that violent, demon-haunted world, with its narrow, walled streets; heavy use of slaves; and wealthy nobles and viziers.

In addition to its use of *Arabian Nights*, *Horse* presents themes presented from Homer's *Odyssey* to Twain's *The Prince and the Pauper*. Hwin approaches Aslan much like the Ugly Duckling goes willingly to the swans, willing to be killed by them.

Reflections of Lewis's Writings and Life

Like Shasta, Lewis was enchanted by the North. Norse myth left him with a sense of mystery and awe over what he called "Northernness." He also knew what it felt like to be snubbed by other children, as Shasta experienced.

The Least You Need to Know

- *Horse* gives good insight into the relationships between Narnia and Archenland (allies), and Narnia and Calormen (enemies), and the role Aslan plays in other lands.

- *Horse* is background material, a story of events from the reign of the Pevensie children, not an essential part of the main story line in the *Chronicles*.

- In *Horse*, we learn that being free is not enough; one must live nobly and grant freedom to others to be truly free.

Chapter 12

The Magician's Nephew

In This Chapter

- The background to the rest of the *Chronicles:* Narnia's existence, Aslan, and other important characters
- The creation of Narnia, and the evil waiting to hurt the new land
- Good and bad magic, and good and bad magicians

Where did Narnia come from, anyway? What is its earliest history? How did the wardrobe get to be magical, and why is that lamppost out there in the middle of nowhere? Readers wondered such questions, so Lewis decided to write the story of how it all began.

Before he could finish telling of Narnia's creation, he wrote all the rest of the tales of its entire history. This book took the longest to write; several others were written at the same time it was coming together. But finally we get back to where it all started … and the seeds of evil that were in Narnia before its sun rose on that very first day.

Fast Facts

The Magician's Nephew, written in 1949–1954 and published in 1955, is chronologically the first of *The Chronicles of Narnia*. It is a prequel to the first book in the series, *The Lion, the Witch and the Wardrobe*. We get to go "behind the scenes" to many people, places, and events of later books—even meeting *Wardrobe*'s Professor Kirke as a young boy, Digory, who is exploring unknown worlds with his neighbor, Polly. (Who would have thought the professor could ever be so impetuous as he was at times in this book?) Lewis used the title *Polly and Digory* as he wrote it.

Narnia's creation, and how an individual's good and bad choices affect other people, is in focus here. It's a very good look at beauty, but also at corruption due to pride and the use of the wrong kind of power.

Navigating Narnia

The Magician's Nephew is dedicated to the Kilmer family. There's a very good reason not all their names were mentioned— there are a lot of them! Several letters in *Letters to Children*, published after Lewis's death, were addressed to the eight children who had been born when this book was published and dedicated to them.

Who Will We Meet?

The characters in this volume are plentiful and diverse. Keep your hat on because we're going to go fast as we meet the most important ones. (Well, take your hat off when we introduce you.) Let's look at who they are and why they're important to this story.

Digory and Polly

Our first look at these two children sees them as unlikely heroes and improbable friends. Digory's face is dirty from crying and rubbing it with grimy hands. Polly doesn't seem inclined to like him. But she understands his tears when she finds out that his mother lies at the point of death.

After the encounter in the garden, the two children are friends, and they are off to explore. Although their planned exploration is limited to an attic and a vacant house, they end up in two unexplored worlds, a dying old world and a fresh young world on its creation day. Like Hansel and Gretel, they will soon meet a witch. Like Dorothy in Oz, they will soon meet a lion. They will also be at the whim of an evil magician. They might have been smarter to stay home.

Digory is a flawed hero, a young man who's brave and compassionate, but who's also fairly stubborn. Once he has made up his mind to do something, good or bad, he'll do it. Polly is in some ways the more adventurous of the two. But she's the one who remembers important things, like marking the magical pool that is the point of connection with our world so she and Digory won't spend the rest of their lives jumping into pools trying to find London again.

When we see Digory as an adult in *Wardrobe*, we see that he has learned to listen to others, that he values truthfulness, and that he can guide others without bullying them.

Digory's Uncle Andrew

Uncle Andrew is evil, cruel, and thoroughly self-absorbed. But he's also a buffoon with limited power, and nobody respects or likes him—at least, nobody in this book does. Digory calls him "mad." Whether actually insane or merely evil, he is interested in no one but himself, yet unwilling to take personal risks. Dabbling in magic, he accidentally gets more than he bargains for when he comes face to face with Aslan. But by that time, he has so immersed himself in evil and lies that he cannot even see Aslan as more than a common lion.

Andrew's magic is actually more "science" than magic. To help his experiment, Uncle Andrew tricks Polly by giving her a "gift" of one of the rings he has made. Somehow he has failed to mention that they are magic rings and that she will disappear from this world when she touches one. As Andrew expects, Digory is enough of a gentleman to follow Polly to bring her home. Not that Andrew really cares whether the little girl gets home safely, but he does care very much to find out whether his experiment has been a success.

Uncle Andrew had perhaps the last living fairy godmother (to be honest, she was only part fairy), but she was evil—a fairy witch. She left a box to him, with his promise that he would destroy it unopened, that gives him the ability to work magic that he couldn't work on his own. Fairy godmothers are usually helpful to the young people in their care, but fairies are often evil (for example, the fairies in *Sleeping Beauty* and in George MacDonald's *Little Daylight*). We can only guess whether Uncle Andrew's godmother knew he would use her gift for evil.

Navigating Narnia

Uncle Andrew resembles "Oldie," the cruel headmaster of Lewis's prep school. The physical description fits, and a letter Lewis wrote as a teen said that Oldie would make a memorable villain. In *Joy*, he says boys on vacation from school would rather talk of a villain who had power over them as a buffoon than an ogre. Here, Lewis treats an ogre as a buffoon.

The Evil Queen Jadis (Duck!)

Digory awakens a proud, fierce, powerful witch, Jadis, from an enchanted sleep in Charn, a world where she is the only living inhabitant. (That's because she killed everyone else and then put herself into a charmed sleep, so don't waste too much time feeling sorry for her.) Through a series of unfortunate events, the Witch ends up in London and then in Narnia, where she poses a grave danger to the new land.

Is Jadis the White Witch of *Wardrobe*? We're not told here, but are given several hints: the tree Digory plants will protect Narnia from Jadis for a long period to come, but eventually she will cause great harm. Aslan says he will make sure that most of the hurt falls on himself. When she eats the silver apple in the garden, her face becomes white as salt. We have a tall, white witch bent on Narnia's destruction, but limited for now in her power to act. But in *Wardrobe*, the note in Tumnus's cave is signed with Jadis's name.

Navigating Narnia

Jadis has destroyed her world by means of a secret weapon: the Deplorable Word. World War II was still a vivid memory when Lewis wrote, and he seemed to be hinting at atomic warfare. To make the hint stronger, Aslan tells the children that someone in our world may develop a similar evil that can destroy our whole world.

A Brave London Cabby

Frank is the cabby whose hansom (a two-wheeled, horse-drawn carriage) is stolen by the Witch and used to plunder the shops of other respectable businessman. (Did we mention Jadis wanted to become empress over England and that she thought ordinary laws were only for ordinary people?) Frank's cab is destroyed when the Witch has a collision with a lamppost. (Notice the lamppost; we'll meet it again in Narnia.)

Frank ends up in Narnia as well—and finds it much better suited to himself and his horse than London is. Aslan calls Frank's wife, Nellie, to join him, and apparently they live happily ever after. Even his horse approvingly notices the change in Frank that comes from a few hours in Narnia. Frank and Nellie (Helen) become the very first king and queen of Narnia. (In *Wardrobe*, we are told that all true kings and queens of Narnia must be human.) In his science-fiction book *Perelandra*, Lewis chose to populate Perelandra (Venus) with a man and a woman who had not yet chosen evil. Frank and Nellie are imperfect human beings, but they want to do what is right. With the introduction of Jadis to the new world, it was too late to look for perfection in Narnia anyway.

An ordinary but honest and hard-working man, Frank is a good candidate for patient leadership of a new land peopled with talking beasts. Nellie is his quiet, humble, equally hard-working companion in the task.

Our First Look at Aslan

A dark land with nothing growing on it—nothing at all. That's everyone's first impression of Narnia. But soon the visitors from London can hear singing, wilder and sweeter than anything they have ever heard, and seeming to come from all directions at once; the singer is, of course, Aslan. The two evil magicians in Digory and Polly's party (that would be the Witch Jadis and Uncle Andrew) hate what they see and hear. Everyone else is in awe as Aslan's singing brings Narnia to life.

The Witch has an iron bar from the lamppost with her, and she makes a rather foolish attempt on Aslan's life. The bar doesn't hurt Aslan when the Witch hurls it; it bounces off his forehead, and he continues walking and singing. Did you ever wonder where the lamppost in the middle of nowhere in Narnia came from? The ground is so fertile in this new land that the bar sprouts into a baby lamp. Aslan is able to thwart intended evil and even turn it into good, as was said of God working in the life of the patriarch Joseph in Genesis 50:15–21.

Talking Animals—and a Winged Horse

Aslan chooses some animals to become talking beasts. He warns them that the honor depends on their not returning to the wild ways of their lowlier cousins. (This warning is fulfilled several times in the *Chronicles*, including *Battle*, when a talking cat loses his power of speech after using it to deceive others.) Talking animals are responsible for caring for the nontalking beasts.

The cabby's horse, Strawberry, is singled out for the special privilege not only of being a talking horse, but of becoming a flying horse as well, rechristened Fledge. He is sent to help Digory on a mission for Aslan. Of course, Polly wants to go along. Aslan gives Digory a lion kiss before he leaves, lending him the necessary courage and strength. I (Cheryl) admit I wish I could be Digory at that moment.

What Should We Watch For?

Nephew is packed full of things we need to know about Narnia—and about life. Here are a few things Lewis wouldn't want you to miss.

The Self-Justification of Evil

Bumbling fool Uncle Andrew and the Witch Jadis are both evil. Although one is extraordinarily powerful and one is working magic on the coattails of another, their perspectives on life are similar. Both proudly think themselves above ordinary people and outside the reach of laws and morality that apply to others. They are frighteningly self-focused, sure of their own importance, and totally unconcerned with what happens to other people. And both heartily dislike Aslan because he is good.

But the Witch and the second-rate magician are not the only characters who bring about evil. Not until Aslan confronts Digory directly does he admit that he made a deliberate choice to do what he knew to be wrong—a choice that hurts everyone around him and brings great evil to Narnia, in the form of the Witch. Even small evils can have serious consequences. Fortunately, he learns his lesson and resists his next big temptation, this one from the Witch herself.

Aslan's Creativity and His Character

Readers who have explored other books in the series already know and love Aslan. But here we get a couple of fresh new pictures of the great lion. First, we see him as a joyful, inventive creator, an artist. We also see his compassion in the tears for Digory's mother. He rules and guides, loving his new creatures and protecting them. But he's not too busy for personal encounters with visitors from our world or for jokes from his exuberant young creatures.

Magic and Myth

Tolkien's mythic *Silmarillion* tells of a world created through a symphony. The book was not published until after Tolkien's death, but Lewis read nearly everything Tolkien wrote as he wrote it. And the animals coming up from the earth in expanding, bursting lumps of dirt? John Milton's *Paradise Lost* has much the same image.

The Contentment That Comes from Doing the Right Thing

The cabby and his wife have a simple life, in a city they'd rather not live in. (They're country folk.) But there's peace and goodness in them and not in the grasping, wealthier Uncle Andrew.

Digory faces great temptation to take something that's off limits—and he could justify it if he did so because his desire is for another, his dying mother. Although the temptation to pluck an extra fruit from the tree of youth is strong, he resists. He can look Aslan in the eye afterward and know that he made the right choice. The best part is Aslan's willing gift of an apple Digory can take home lawfully.

One of the sweetest but simplest biblical allusions is Aslan's "Well done," when Digory brings back the fruit. This comes from one of Jesus' parables illustrating heavenly reward (Matthew 25:21–23). This is one of three times in the *Chronicles* that Aslan blesses a person with "Well done." (The others are King Tirian in *Battle*, for leading his people wisely up until the end; and Edmund in *Caspian*, for trusting Aslan enough to see him when he was invisible to everyone else except Lucy.) Normally, we don't follow Narnia's visitors very long after they slip back into our world, but in *Nephew* we do because we need to see some very significant things. Most involve that magic apple Aslan gave to Digory for his mother. First, it did heal her. Second, Digory buried the core in the backyard, and a tree grew from it (very quickly, too). The apples on it weren't magic, but the tree seemed to remember Narnia. Years later, when the tree blew over in a storm, the professor had a wardrobe made from the wood. And guess what happened to that wardrobe? (See *Wardrobe*, where it becomes an entry point to Narnia.) Oh, and the children buried the rings around the tree so no one would ever use them again.

The apple of youth, present in many myths and in *Nephew*, could also be a mirror of the Tree of Life in the Garden of Eden. Adam and Eve are barred from access to it after eating of the forbidden Tree of the Knowledge of Good and Evil. The Tree of Life next shows up in Revelation 22:2, in which perfected citizens of heaven are given free access to it.

The Self-Inflicted Hurt in Evil

Uncle Andrew is proud and selfish—and miserable. While the others are reveling in creation's song and the animals coming to life around them, Andrew convinces himself that he hears only a growling lion and sees dangerous wild animals wanting to eat him. All he notices of value in Narnia is a potential to make money. One can only pity him, although he is the victim of his own choices.

How Good or Evil Choices Affect Other People

One boy's seemingly small choice to do the wrong thing, hitting a bell, hurt his new friend, Polly, and all of Narnia, when it brought a witch to life. It also resulted in great expense for several people in London who were victims of Jadis's rampage and her thefts.

Uncle Andrew's selfish choices send two young children into unknown other worlds, without any assurance they will be safe. He has taken advantage of his sister for so long that she no longer trusts him, and the children actively avoid him. He doesn't care about being a good uncle to his nephew, whose father is overseas and mother is dying.

God Sightings

Digory's mother doesn't come into the story directly until the very end. Aslan has sent her a magic apple to relieve her suffering and prolong her life. In Lewis's Christian worldview, suffering is not always bad. Those who suffer can learn compassion for others and trust in God's strengthening. But for Digory's sake, Aslan heals his mother.

But good choices also affect others. Digory brings the Witch, but he also brings the apple that will keep her away—the apples on the tree that grows from it will repel her. He also takes home an apple that heals his mother. The animals and people work together for the coronation of their new king and queen. Each citizen contributes his own talents, from the moles' digging to the dwarfs' ability to work with fine metal.

A Child's-Eye View

Much comes into this story that is perfectly suited to a child's fancy, whether hints of other beloved stories, animals and humor, or earthy touches of good things in their own world.

We see things that are "cool": the last fairy godmother; a toffee tree growing from planted candy; laughing, joking animals and an argument between an elephant and a bulldog as to the proper length of a nose; animals popping out of the earth; and a wise, kind horse that grows wings.

Nephew also has scary elements, which children tend to like: the collapsing buildings in Charn as the children and the Witch race out; the Witch herself; Uncle Andrew, who is a cruel but comic character— allowing child readers to distance themselves from the fear of an evil adult.

Many scenes compel awe: the hall of kings and queens in beautiful clothing and costly jewels; the creation with its singing stars and newly formed multitude of animals; and, of course, Aslan, the powerful but sympathetic lion who cannot be injured by an iron bar flung at him at close range. (The White Witch in *Wardrobe* will injure him with his permission, but even then Aslan wins.)

Children will sympathize with Digory's mother's illness, which threatens to end in her death, and feel his relief when she is healed. As scary as the Witch is, her desired transportation in London hints of an exciting history from a child's perspective: she requests a chariot, a flying carpet, or a well-trained dragon. One suspects she wouldn't appreciate them if she got them, but the child reader would.

Series-Wide Issues Lewis Develops

Lewis looks at the power of desire: desires for adventure, for a mother's healing, for that which looks and smells good like the silver apple, for illegitimate power. *Nephew* illustrates the hazard of settling for the wrong things—in the case of Uncle Andrew, that means greedily wanting the fertility of Narnia for its money-making potential and not wanting Narnia itself, and definitely not wanting Aslan.

Sayings and Sound Advice

Aslan warns about attempting to be stupider than one actually is. It saddens the lion to see how well humans protect themselves from what will do them good. When Uncle Andrew refuses to see Aslan's goodness or hear anything other than beastly roaring, Aslan tells the children that he has made his own choices. Because Andrew will not heed, Aslan can put him in a restful sleep but has nothing else he can give him. A similar inability to receive Aslan's blessings is shown at the end of Narnia, when the dwarfs in *Battle* refuse to see the lovely banquet Aslan has given, imagining that they are eating hay and old turnips and drinking dirty water from a trough.

Narnian Themes

In *Nephew*, the contentment from doing one's duty shows up in Digory's going after the apple, but also in his persistent desire to remove the Witch from London.

We know good and bad characters partly by their compassion to beasts and those in lower standing, or their lack of it.

Again and again in Narnia, we see Aslan's power to draw good people to himself to be made better and to repel those who prefer evil. Frank, the honest cab driver, says that he "almost" knows Aslan already, a hint developed in other books that Aslan is a picture of Jesus Christ.

King Frank and Queen Helen are given their royal charge: to rule, to name, to do justice, and to protect those under their care. In some ways, they are like Adam and Eve, the first couple in our world, and their assignment is similar. King Frank isn't sure he's up to the task of being king, but his honest humility is matched by his appropriately frank determination to do his best.

Also, we see in Digory and in Uncle Andrew that a person cannot learn and grow until he takes responsibility for the wrong he has done. Eustace in *Voyage* probably presents the series' best example of one who finds peace only when he admits that he himself is the problem.

Religious References, Mythic Echoes

As this book goes to the very heart of all stories, creation, it is not surprising that it echoes many earlier stories.

Biblical Parallels

Obviously, many elements of this tale come from the Genesis accounts of Creation and the Fall. Even the order of Aslan's creation is similar: first the stars and the sun, then plants, then animals, and then intelligent life. Aslan's top creation is talking animals and humanlike beings such as dwarfs and fauns, not people; humans come from outside. A threat also comes from outside the creation, tempting an inhabitant to disobedience in the form of eating forbidden fruit.

We see Aslan as creator and loving ruler. He is opposed by a tempter who comes in seeking to destroy the good creation or tempt its residents into evil. The tempter is very powerful—but not nearly as powerful as the creator.

Narnian Dictionary

The Fall is the account from Genesis 3 in which Adam and Eve, the first humans, chose to sin. They had been given complete freedom with only one prohibition: not to eat from one tree in the center of the Garden of Eden. (Sound familiar?) A serpent tempted them, and they ate the forbidden fruit, plunging all mankind into a bent toward sin.

Job 38:6–7 has a beautiful image of "morning stars" singing at creation—apparently not literal stars, but angels. Aslan's living, singing stars may well be patterned after this beautiful image.

Egyptian

In the private garden to which Aslan sends Digory for an apple, the special tree sits in the center. The smell of its fruit is enticing, almost impossible to resist. As Digory gives one last longing look at the tree, he sees a multicolored bird in its top. The bird does not speak and only seems to peek at him, but it is enough to know someone is watching. As stated specifically in *Battle*, the bird is a phoenix, associated with longevity and immortality. What better guard for the tree of youth?

Greek

Several of the beings Aslan created have their origins in Greek myths. These include dryads, or wood nymphs, which have already been seen at play in several Narnian chronicles, among them *Prince Caspian*. The river god and his daughters, the beautiful naiads, are also seen on this first day of Narnia's existence. Plato's legendary Atlantis even appears, as the place where the box holding the otherworldly dirt was made. Fledge is a humble, lovable version of Pegasus, a winged horse of Greek mythology and also one of the constellations in our night sky.

In Greek mythology, the Garden of the Hesperides contained a tree of golden apples guarded by a dragon. Hercules killed the dragon to obtain the golden apples.

Arthurian

Uncle Andrew's part-fairy godmother, Mrs. Lefay, is clearly evil, in spite of Andrew's high praise of her. The owner of the box of soil from which the rings were made, she plays a peripheral but foundational role in the story. Her name is a hint of King Arthur's half-sister and enemy, sorceress Morgan LeFay.

Norse

Giants and dwarfs come from Norse mythology, one of Lewis's earliest favorite forms. The god Loki stole treasure, including a magic ring, from the dwarf Andvari. The dwarfs in *Nephew* prove their worth at the end of the story as they create the crowns of their new king and queen. In *Battle*, the dwarfs are for the dwarfs and will not be ruled by another, but here they are humble, willing citizens and workers.

Dropping Hints: Literary Allusions

Lewis seemed to delight at dropping hints of his favorite authors into his books, and this story is full of them.

All Those Other Authors

The opening page mentions that this story took place in the days of the Bastable children (creations of E. Nesbit in *The Treasure Seekers* and sequels) and Sherlock Holmes. A different Nesbit story, *The Story of the Amulet*, even lent Lewis one of his more memorable scenes. In that book, children brought a queen from ancient Babylon home with them to London (not meaning to do so, of course), where she caused a riot.

Algernon Blackwood's book *The Education of Uncle Paul* (1909) included a location that enchanted the teenage Lewis, a quiet forest and a calm river, Beyond-World, which sounds remarkably like the Wood Between the Worlds, the link between our world and Charn, Narnia, and nobody knows how many other worlds.

Furthermore, as Lewis worked through the years on helping Tolkien shape his story of Middle-Earth (*The Lord of the Rings*), its elves and hobbits, and a ring that causes its wearer to disappear, Lewis wrote his own tale with children and rings that cause them to vanish … and reappear in a different world. E. Nesbit's book *The Enchanted Castle* also includes a ring that makes its wearer invisible.

Reflections of Lewis's Writings and Life

The opening scene has much of Lewis's childhood in it, from the attic with tunnels and small doors like he had in Little Lea, his childhood home, to the stiff Eton collars boys had to wear, which he wore as a child and hated. Lewis tells us of nastier schools and nicer sweets than the readers experience.

As a child, Lewis prayed that God would heal his mother, even resurrect her. Much to his sorrow, God said no. In this tale, Lewis has the power to give a boy back his mother—and to let us see the compassion and tears in Aslan's eyes as he hears the boy's grief-stricken request.

The Least You Need to Know

◉ *The Magician's Nephew* is the earliest story of Narnia—the story of its creation.

◉ *Nephew* gives us key background to features in Narnia that are otherwise unexplained: the wardrobe, how the Professor knows of Narnia, the lamppost in Lantern Waste, and probably the White Witch.

◉ Magic is an important part of Narnia, but *Nephew* illustrates magic's evil possibilities as well as its good ones.

Chapter 13

The Last Battle

In This Chapter

- Narnia's final days and closing battles
- Aslan's plans for the future of loyal Narnians and others who love him
- A last look at nearly every major character from earlier books

From the very beginning of *Battle*, we know Narnia is about to meet its end. That makes this book bittersweet—we want to see what happens, but we also want to linger in Narnia, and it hurts to see it destroyed.

Tirian, Narnia's last king, is on the side of good. But he is young, and sinister forces beyond his understanding have made their way into Narnia. He longs to believe that Aslan is indeed in Narnia again—but the being who seems to have come to Narnia is not the Aslan of the old tales. In fact, he is a false Aslan, under the control of others who have their own selfish and even sinister motives.

Back in England, the friends of Narnia, the children from the various Narnia stories (minus Susan) are meeting, concerned that something is going wrong in the land they love. Their future is about to intersect with Narnia's future in a different way than they expect. Narnia's last days are sad, but its future is wonderful.

Fast Facts

Titles Lewis considered for this book include *The Last King of Narnia* and *Night Falls on Narnia*.

Battle is the only book with no dedication, and it was published last, in 1956. *Battle* won the Carnegie Medal—given yearly since 1936 for the best children's book published in the United Kingdom. Some believe that *Battle* won the medal because it was the last in the series, and thus its win represented the completed series. Lewis made sure his illustrator, Pauline Baynes, understood that the win was an honor to her illustrations as well as his text.

Magic and Myth

Illustrator Pauline Baynes was born in England in 1922. She drew the art for Tolkien's *Farmer Giles of Ham*, published in 1949. Lewis liked her work well enough to ask her to illustrate *The Chronicles of Narnia*. She was young and not very experienced, and if you compare the drawings from one book to another, it's clear she was improving as the series progressed.

It has been more than a year Earth time since *Chair*, 200 years in Narnia. Throughout the story, Tirian and his friends, the loyal Narnians, experience rising and falling hope. The deceivers have the upper hand in the entire book, although the Narnians have several reasons to expect that things are about to turn. Not until the end do the loyal Narnians see victory, when death itself is turned to life.

Who Will We Meet?

For most of this book, we will be meeting new people. Partway through, we will see children who have been in Narnia before, and Jill and Eustace rejoin us. But Aslan will not appear until the end. At the end, be ready—nearly everyone of any significance from the entire series will be on hand to give encore appearances. (That's Lewis's way of letting us know they did all live happily ever after.)

Puzzle the Donkey and Shift the Ape

The first creatures we meet seem to be friends—a donkey, Puzzle, and an ape, Shift. The ape is clearly in charge, and a master at manipulating the gullible, gentle donkey to get him to do menial tasks for Shift's benefit. Puzzle is really Shift's servant, not his friend.

Shift pretends to speak for Aslan in an audacious plan of dressing the donkey in a lion skin. So a false Aslan is born, and Puzzle soon is in cahoots with the Calormenes for the benefit of the Calormenes.

The loyal Narnians don't want to fight against Aslan, if this really is Aslan, so they are distressed and confused. Soon Shift dresses in clothes—the only talking animal in Narnia to do so—and pretends to be a man. Shift betrays his own disbelief in Aslan, saying to Puzzle "the real Aslan, *as you call him*" (emphasis added).

At the end of the world, Tirian hurls Shift into the stable, where Tash claims him as prey. Inside the stable—or, rather, the new Narnia—Puzzle is afraid to meet Aslan. Although he was duped by another, he did what ought not to be done. But Puzzle is the first one Aslan calls to himself. Aslan speaks privately to him, and he is restored. Puzzle does bear some responsibility for going along with the scheme, but he never had evil intentions and his love for Aslan is genuine. But those who have chosen evil are judged as fully responsible for that evil.

King Tirian, the Last King

All other kings we've seen in Narnia have been shown to us at the very beginning of their reign. Tirian is still a young man, in his early twenties, but he has been in wars. Tirian is sixth or seventh in descent from Rilian of *Chair* (an inconsistency). He is about to see Narnia's last battle, a losing one. He is introduced to readers as "the last of the Kings of Narnia." He is a good king who deeply cares for his subjects.

King Tirian is happy to hear numerous reports that Aslan has been seen in Narnia. Yet the reports become more and more puzzling. He soon hears that talking trees have been felled and talking horses harnessed and whipped, on this Aslan's orders. When a dryad's tree is being felled while she is talking to Tirian, she runs, crying out, "Woe, woe, woe!" like an angel in Revelation 8:13 calling to the inhabitants of Earth. King Tirian visits Lantern Waste, where he finds that half the crowd are men from Calormen. He continues to hope that the real Aslan is in Narnia long after it should be obvious Aslan is not, because his desire for Aslan is so deep. He is a young king and out of his element in these horrible final days. But he does the right thing when he calls out to Aslan. The final battle is hopeless, but soon Tirian will meet the real Aslan. Aslan tells Tirian "Well done" for standing firm in Narnia's darkest hour. In Aslan's country, Tirian looks at the clean kings and queens and feels bad about coming in covered with the filth of battle—but looks at himself and sees that he, too, has been cleansed and freshly dressed. He has been provided with clothes by another, just as Eustace was in *Voyage*, and just as the Christian will be someday according to Revelation 19:7–8.

Jewel the Unicorn and Roonwit the Centaur

Jewel the unicorn is King Tirian's best friend. The two grew up together, and they saved each other's life in the wars. They are affectionate with each other and trust each other implicitly. Roonwit is another counselor to the king, a centaur who has seen very bad tidings in the stars. He is sure that the reports of Aslan are not true; the stars promise bad rather than good, and the stars never lie. Tirian trusts Roonwit, but he doesn't really hear him, as he wants to believe that the lion sightings are really Aslan. According to Matthew 24, in the last days, even believers will be nearly led astray by false idols as we head into the end of the age.

Roonwit is sent to gather warriors for King Tirian and Narnia. When Roonwit himself ends up dead, Narnia's doom is evident. From Tirian's perspective, at this point Narnia is no more, although he is willing to fight to his last breath. Tirian commands the children to return to their own world, but it is not within their power to do so.

One of the most famous of centaurs is, like Roonwit, an adviser on important matters: the centaur Cheron in Greek mythology, who taught Asclepius the art of healing. Lewis's centaurs are stargazers and prophets, but their wisdom is deeply respected.

Unicorns symbolize purity, and Jewel is clearly on the side of right—although he isn't a gentle pacifist, but a seasoned warrior. Lewis explains that unicorns are brave in battle, loyal, and very powerful fighters: a unicorn can use his horn, his front feet, and his teeth all at the same time. But when Puzzle is brought away from the stable, Jewel shows his value as a friend. He helps Puzzle feel comfortable by talking to him about things they both understand, like grass and sugar and care of one's hoofs. He's a unicorn, but he's not an elitist, and he isn't too good to associate with a common donkey.

Ginger the Cat

Ginger is very sly. He seems to be an ordinary talking cat, although he is in league with the Calormenes and Shift the ape. Shift may even report to him; this is suggested as a possibility but never verified. His seeming innocence is used as a tool to draw in other Narnians.

Ginger is an atheist who doesn't believe in Aslan or Tash, but he can use others' beliefs to manipulate them. When the children rescued King Tirian, Ginger explained Tirian's disappearance in religious terms, telling the crowd that he had heard Tirian cursing Aslan, and Aslan had appeared and eaten him.

But he himself is in over his head, fooling with powers he doesn't believe in who are stronger than he is, and he will soon meet his match.

Ginger volunteers to go into the stable to meet Tash. He walks in calmly but comes out in genuine terror, the terror of a common alley cat rather than a talking beast. (We are told later that he was almost eaten by Tash.) He tries to speak but only wails. He has, in fact, lost his power of speech, a punishment foretold at the beginning of Narnia for talking beasts who knowingly choose evil. This terrifies the other talking animals. The Bible tells of the introduction of sin to our planet in a story that includes a talking snake (Genesis 3). Though the snake seems to have been influenced by Satan and perhaps was given the ability to speak by Satan, the snake itself is punished in verses 14–15.

Jill Pole and Eustace Scrubb

Jill and Eustace go to Narnia to help in the crisis. Incidentally, it's the only time in the *Chronicles* that *less* time goes by in Narnia than in our world because the need is dire—a week on Earth is a few minutes in Narnia. They arrive in time to free the king and rescue Jewel, and Jill even explores the barn and rescues Puzzle.

Jill is the best navigator of the party, so she is put in front. She glides silently and almost invisibly, and finds the best view for the king to see what he needs to see.

This is Eustace's third visit to Narnia, placing him after only Lucy and Edmund in number of trips to Narnia. Like Eustace, each of them visits Narnia in three different books, but Lucy went through the wardrobe for two brief visits before her siblings came in, and Edmund for one. And, of course, only the Pevensies had a prolonged stay in Narnia, as they ruled for several years.

Dwarfs

When we first see the dwarfs, a line of them is being taken to the Tisroc's mines in Calormen. Believing themselves to have been sold by Aslan, they are going willingly. Tirian shows them that they have been deceived. Instead of thanking Tirian and fighting on his side, they turn against him and Aslan, and choose to be only for themselves. They choose cunning instead of belief.

Their choice disheartens Tirian. He needs their support in his army. But having been fooled by the false Aslan, they reject the true one. Their war cry becomes "The Dwarfs are for the Dwarfs." It is the beginning of the end for Narnia. Tirian knows he cannot count on anything now.

Dwarfs usually appear in groups in literature: from Snow White's 7 friends to *The Hobbit*'s 13 travelers. So one usually has a choice: have all of them on your side or all of them as your enemies. Dwarfs make formidable enemies, being good with weapons and relatively fearless. Tirian expects his evidence to turn this crowd, but it doesn't work.

One of the saddest scenes in the whole book is when the dwarfs shoot the entire group of talking horses in order to hurt and disillusion Tirian's army. Soon 11 bound dwarfs are thrown into the stable. Even in the stable, they stay in their own little clique. The kings and queens reach out to them, and Aslan does also, but they insist on having their own way.

> **Navigating Narnia**
>
> Tirian is greatly encouraged when one dwarf, Poggin, leaves the other dwarfs to follow his king. Poggin brings them news, cheers them up, and even hunts breakfast the following day.

Rishda Tarkaan

A Calormene captain in league with Shift the ape and Ginger the cat, Rishda does not believe in the Tash he claims to worship. Like his colleagues, he is happy enough to vulgarize Tash and Aslan into "Tashlan." The man and the cat seem to be pulling the strings, telling the ape what to say and how to keep the crowds' obedience and fear.

Rishda is horrified at evidence that Tash really exists and begins frantically trying to serve him to appease his own disbelief. He seeks to drive his enemies into the stable so that he can give them to Tash as an offering. Tirian pulls Rishda into the stable with him, when Rishda is attempting to force Tirian into the stable, and Rishda meets Tash. Aslan sends Tash out of Narnia with Rishda as his lawful prey. Rishda was being religious to fit in with his countrymen and gain power, but his carelessness in choosing a deity proved to be his undoing.

Tash

The Calormenes have called for their god Tash. The deceivers have started combining Aslan's name with that of Tash, calling for Tashlan. No one expects Tash himself to show up, but he does, bringing horror. This god is a demon, with no good wishes for his people.

Tirian and his party see Tash first. He arrives with a hideous, deathly smell, and seems to burn the grass as he passes. He is immense, with the head of a vulture and four arms. One can see through his body, like smoke. It seems cold as he passes.

Tash is much like Nisroch as he is presented in E. Nesbit's *Story of the Amulet*. He also bears much similarity to Lewis's portrayal of the old priest of the goddess Ungit in *Till We Have Faces*. The vile smell of Tash and the burned-over grass as he passes both show up as evil begins to dominate in Charles Williams' *Place of the Lion*, and there we also see a giant bird with a huge beak seeking prey.

That Aslan and Tash are said to be the same being is enough to prove the Aslan of the stable is false. Tirian isn't fooled for a moment about reports that Aslan and Tash are the same being. His unasked question is how Tash, who feeds on the blood of his people, could possibly be the same as Aslan, who rescued his people with his blood. To those who really know Aslan, no one else can be seen as his equal. Lewis, of course, was showing Jesus Christ as superior to all other possible gods, and the one who saved His people by His blood.

Friends of Narnia

In England, the friends of Narnia don't know what is going on in Narnia, but they are sure something is wrong. When King Tirian's face is seen briefly during their meeting, they have that sense of doom confirmed but don't know what is amiss.

God Sightings

It's sad to see that Susan is not among the friends of Narnia. She was too grown-up and too distracted by trivial interests. But Lewis pointed out to letter writers who asked that she is still alive in our world, so there's hope. The Bible likewise says that God gives continued breath to sinners, allowing them further time to repent.

In the circle of seven friends of Narnia are the Professor (Digory Kirke from the very beginning of Narnia, recorded in *Nephew*, and later the Professor in *Wardrobe*) and his friend, Polly Plummer; three of the Pevensie children (all but Susan, who no longer believes in Narnia); and Jill and Eustace, who have traveled to Narnia previously (both of them in *Chair*, Eustace in *Voyage*).

Eustace and Jill are drawn into Narnia to help King Tirian; the rest end up in the new Narnia. Interestingly, Eustace and Jill are crowned as king and queen when they themselves get to the new Narnia. Lucy mourns for Narnia, and Tirian understands her grief.

Aslan asks the children why they do not seem as happy as he means for them to be. They are afraid of being sent away, so Aslan reassures them they have come to stay. They have died in England; this is now their home. And after he tells them that, he looks less and less like a lion. For us, the story of Narnia is coming to an end, but to the children, it is just beginning the first chapter. (They really are about to live happily ever after.)

Aslan

Aslan does not arrive in Narnia during the course of this book; he's waiting to close history on Narnia and to welcome loyal Narnians to his country, the new Narnia.

When the deceivers give the invitation to go into the stable and meet Aslan, the offer brings a rush of animals, in spite of the recent horrors said to have come from Aslan. Tirian reassures his faithful friends that all are between the paws of the true Aslan.

Emeth enters the stable voluntarily, against the wishes of his Tarkaan. He goes in with his head high, his eyes shining, looking solemn. Jewel is impressed with Emeth's demeanor and whispers that he deserves a better god than Tash. When Emeth meets Aslan, he confesses that he has worshipped Tash. But he bows before Aslan and loves him, and rejoices to be called Beloved. Emeth is a sincere believer with noble intentions and pure heart. His name is Hebrew for "truth." Aslan tells him he didn't find Tash because he wasn't really seeking Tash; he was seeking Aslan all along.

Soon the battle is over. Narnia is no more. Aslan closes history by roaring "Time." A whole cycle of events commences, including the awakening of Father Time and the lizardlike creatures that Jill and Eustace found asleep in Underland in *Chair*.

In what seemed like a dream, with no way of knowing whether it lasted for minutes or years, all of Narnia's creatures came in the stable door and looked at Aslan. Those who looked at him in love passed to Aslan's right, into the new Narnia. This correlates with the Bible's description of the final judgment, when believers and unbelievers will be separated, believers on Jesus' right and unbelievers on the left (Matthew 25:31–46). Those who looked at Aslan with fear and hatred passed to his left, into his shadow; the beasts among these ceased to be talking beasts. By this time, the stars had come home to Aslan's country, and their great light made Aslan's shadow huge.

For those who love Aslan, the joys of Aslan's country await: they won't be sent away, won't grow old, won't tire or feel fearful, and won't sin (they can't want wrong things anymore), and time no longer exists. The new Narnia is even more beautiful than the old—the same, only better, unspoiled. The idea of the new Narnia may be based on the concept of heaven as a new Jerusalem, from Hebrews 12:22. (Hebrews was, of course, written to Hebrews—Jews.)

What Should We Watch For?

This final story in Narnia, an *apocalypse*, moves quickly at times, with a story line that almost assumes familiarity with earlier apocalypses. Many of its characters are deceivers as well, so one must watch carefully to see what is happening.

Narnian Dictionary

An **apocalypse** is a story of great disaster, usually associated with the end of the world. The last book of the Bible, Revelation, is also sometimes called the "Apocalypse."

Truth That Is Being Hidden

Narnia is silent at night as the last days arrive, from gloom and fear— yet somehow Narnians still think Aslan is among them.

Roonwit is very direct in his assessment that current events are not a sign that Aslan is in Narnia. The stars do not speak of his presence, but of disaster. Yet Tirian does not really hear him because his desire for Aslan is too strong for him to be easily dissuaded.

Manipulation and Deceit

Narnia's enemies and the false Narnians are able to deceive the nation because Narnians didn't know the truth as well as they should have. This false Aslan doesn't fit anything they know about Aslan, and that should be reason enough to reject him. But the Narnians want to see Aslan, even if he doesn't fit their expectations, and the deceivers are experts at manipulation.

A Talking Beast That Loses Its Speech

Seeing Ginger become an ordinary cat frightened other talking animals who watched the transformation—one of the reasons we are sometimes able to see consequences in the lives of others without having to make bad choices ourselves and take the consequences ourselves.

On the day of creation, Aslan warned that talking beasts could lose their ability to speak. We see several evidences of such in Narnia, including the Lapsed Talking Bear of Stormness in *Horse*. But none is portrayed so vividly or publicly as Ginger, for his defiance of Aslan has been public.

A Child's-Eye View

Old people may look forward to having less creaky joints or being reunited with dead loved ones, but what would a child most value about heaven or Aslan's country? (Other than seeing Christ or Aslan, of course.) Well, it is truly beautiful, with the best elements of different worlds. Children who aren't good athletes (like Lewis) might appreciate not being left behind in a race. In Aslan's country, everyone can keep up with the fastest runners. And fear is a thing of the past, a change every child (and every adult) can relate to on some level.

Nearly all the characters we've met in the *Chronicles* are here, together at last (including Reepicheep and Fledge). Whichever characters are a child's favorite, it's a sweet and unexpected pleasure to meet old friends again.

> **Navigating Narnia**
>
> Water shows up regularly in *Battle*. The lion skin is found at Caldron Pool. The idea of a bad Aslan is like "dry water." The battling loyal Narnians find a comforting trickle and little pool at a white rock. In Aslan's country, we meet Emeth by a clear stream; the Narnians swim *up* the great waterfall; and Aslan bounds to meet them like a living waterfall.

Series-Wide Issues Lewis Develops

Roonwit is waiting for the newcomers in the new Narnia and instructs them to come "further up, come further in!" They are insiders here and can fully immerse themselves as citizens of this new land prepared for them. The Pevensies' first stay in Narnia began with the instruction by Mr. Beaver to come "further in." Here the instruction is repeated—but now they are here to stay.

Sayings and Sound Advice

When Tash turns out to be real, contrary to the expectations of those who have called him into Narnia, Poggin wisely says, "People shouldn't call for demons unless they really mean what they say." Good advice in an era when supernatural things have become a game or party entertainment!

In *Battle*, rather than taking chances, the true Narnians are accepting the adventure Aslan sends. That is what it means to live by faith—to see that God is really in charge, and to rest in Him and trust that He is really good, even in hard times. Even when we don't know the future, we can trust it to God, if we belong to Him.

Narnian Themes

The lamb (an innocent child) knows enough to see that Aslan and Tash can't be the same. The deceivers make fun of the lamb but do not answer it.

The stable door is really the door into Aslan's country—even suffering and death are under Aslan's control. The stable and the wardrobe are both bigger inside than outside. In *Wardrobe*, all of Narnia was, in one sense, inside the wardrobe; here, all of Aslan's country seems to be inside the stable.

As is common in Narnia, people find in Aslan's country a kind of happiness and wonder that makes you serious. The desire for Aslan's country is fulfilled at last.

Tirian is more amazed by Jill and Eustace's presence than they are surprised at being in Narnia. They have been here before. Although Tirian has heard of creatures from another world, he has never seen any. Such a concept, the unexpected arrival of people in Narnia from Earth, is used repeatedly in the *Chronicles*.

Religious References, Mythic Echoes

The closing chapters of *Battle*, including the destruction of Narnia, reflect Christian *eschatology*, but also Norse myth and other Armageddons.

Narnian Dictionary

Eschatology is the study of end times, the end of the earth or the universe. In Christian theology, eschatology usually looks primarily at the last book of the Bible, Revelation, but it also looks at other books, including the unusual visions in the Old Testament book of Daniel.

Biblical Parallels

Much about *Battle*'s apocalypse is based on Scripture. Shift is an anti-christ (an imitation of the real thing, coming to deceive—as in Matthew 24:24). The white stone that Tirian and the others found during the last desperate stages of the battle, and from which they drank refreshing waters, is probably a combination of the white stone given as a reward for service in Revelation 21:7 and the rock from which Moses called forth water in Exodus 17:5–6. (In 1 Corinthians 10:4, we learn that the rock represents Christ.)

Peter shuts and locks the stable door leading back to the old Narnia—a hint of the keys of the kingdom of heaven symbolically given to the apostle Peter in Matthew 16:18.

"Save us, Shift, from Aslan" may be an allusion to Revelation 6:16, in which people of the last days end up calling to the mountains to hide them and save them from the wrath of the Lamb (Jesus).

But there is a sense in which it is good to fear God, as those who love Aslan still fear him. The fear of the Lord is the beginning of knowledge, according to Proverbs 1:7, and helps us depart from evil, as seen in Proverbs 16:6.

Tirian and Jewel's rage-provoked murder is like Moses killing an Egyptian in a quick-tempered way to seek justice for wrongs against his people (Exodus 2:11–12).

Tirian is surprised that Aslan's whole country seems to be inside the stable, but Lucy tells him that once in our world, a humble stable held something bigger than our whole world. She means, of course, when Jesus was a baby in a stable.

Greek

Unicorns vary in literature, sometimes being a cross between a horse and a goat or a mix of other animals. Most often today they are shown as a white horse with one horn, representing purity (and sometimes even representing Jesus). The Greek historian Ctesias, around 400 B.C., may be the first person to mention a one-horned horse.

Arthurian

The kings and queens of Narnia are assembled in the new Narnia, with others among them who had not been kings and queens in Narnia itself. They no longer carry swords, of course, as they no longer need them. But they still retain the chivalrous air of those in King Arthur's court, along with the authority of the true high king, Aslan.

Norse

The final end of Narnia is based more on the Norse myth of the end of the world, Ragnarök (sometimes called the "Twilight of the Gods") than on the biblical perspective of the end of our world. Ragnarök is preceded by a great winter, Fimbulwinter—three successive heavy winters without intervening summers—and accompanied by a rising sea.

Dropping Hints: Literary Allusions

Battle contains pieces from many sources, including books by Lewis's friends and themes he has used previously himself. Let's look at several of them.

All Those Other Authors

Aesop's fables include a tale of a donkey in lion skin who gets away with his disguise until he brays. *Battle's* lion-skinned donkey, Puzzle, stays silent and lets someone "wiser" do the talking.

When the friends of Narnia arrive in the new Narnia, slowly they realize they are in the *real* Narnia. The one they have known is but a shadow or copy of this one, like the story told by Plato of the shadows in the cave being mistaken for real objects.

The dwarfs' inability to see in the stable is like Curdie in *The Princess and the Goblin*. Curdie's friend Irene has taken him to meet her fairy grandmother. Curdie cannot see anything attractive at all on his first visit. (Later he does.)

Reflections of Lewis's Writings and Life

The Narnian marching song that Tirian hums as he is walking with the children from our world comes from Lewis's "March for Drum, Trumpet, and Twenty-one Giants" published in the November 4, 1953, edition of *Punch*, a British literary and humor magazine (and also as "Narnian Suite" in his posthumously published *Poems*, where a trotting march for dwarfs is added).

In the 1950s, Lewis had a huge tomcat called Ginger, which he mentioned in a February 22, 1958, letter printed in *Letters to an American Lady*. Lewis never says whether the cat was impressed by being immortalized as a sly, atheistic trickster.

The Least You Need to Know

⊗ *The Last Battle* takes us to the very end of Narnian history; Narnia as we know it is doomed, and eternity is about to commence.

⊗ The Calormenes have been searching for many years for a way to destroy Narnia; in league with traitors from within Narnia, and even a false Aslan, they find their opportunity.

⊗ Aslan's country turns out to contain the best parts of Narnia and Earth, and in *Battle* we meet most of the good characters from earlier *Chronicles*, waiting in Aslan's country.

Selected Additional Resources

Books About Narnia

Brown, Devin. *Inside Narnia: A Guide to Exploring The Lion, the Witch and the Wardrobe.* Grand Rapids: Baker, 2005.

A very readable, user-friendly book on Narnia.

Downing, David C. *Into the Wardrobe: C. S. Lewis and the Narnian Chronicles.* San Francisco: Jossey-Bass, 2005.

Downing's book is an excellent look at the background to Narnia, including humor and Narnian names. An appendix covers potentially unfamiliar beings, places, and words from each book.

Lindskoog, Kathryn. *Journey into Narnia*. Pasadena, Calif.: Hope Publishing, 1998.

> Lewis himself read and approved the material in the first half of this book, entitled "The Lion of Judah in Never-Never Land," one of the first books written about what Lewis was doing with Narnia. The second half of the book is a book-by-book explanation of each book's themes, characters, and more.

Manguel, Alberto, and Gianni Guadalupi. *Dictionary of Imaginary Places*. New York: Harcourt Brace & Company, 2000.

> A travelogue exploring many literary imaginary worlds and treating them as real places, based on the authors' own descriptions. Complete with maps of many familiar fantasy worlds. Narnia and several of its principle locations are included.

Books About C. S. Lewis and His World

Carpenter, Humphrey. *The Inklings: C. S. Lewis, J. R. R. Tolkien, Charles Williams, and Their Friends*. Boston: Houghton Mifflin, 1979.

> A good look at Lewis's literary friendships in the informal literary group called the Inklings.

Dorsett, Lyle W., and Marjorie Lamp Mead, eds. *C. S. Lewis: Letters to Children*. New York: Simon & Schuster, 1995.

> A good, quick read of letters to children who wrote to Lewis, and to his goddaughter; excellent background to Narnia and Lewis.

Hooper, Walter, ed. *Letters of C. S. Lewis*. San Diego: Harcourt Brace & Company, 1988.

> An excellent, fun resource, with hundreds of letters to Lewis's friends, family, and fans; complete with biographical notes by Lewis's brother, Warren.

Jacobs, Alan. *The Narnian: The Life and Imagination of C. S. Lewis.* San Francisco: Harper Collins, 2006.

A new biography of Lewis; good, though it relies heavily on other sources.

Kilby, Clyde S., and Marjorie Lamp Mead. *Brothers and Friends: The Diaries of Major Warren Hamilton Lewis.* San Francisco: Harper & Row, 1982.

The life of Lewis as seen by his brother and best friend, Warren. The two brothers lived together most of their life.

Lewis, C. S. *Surprised by Joy.* New York: Harcourt Brace Jovanovich, 1955.

Lewis's autobiography, focusing on his search for meaning in life.

Martindale, Wayne, and Jerry Root, eds. *The Quotable Lewis.* Wheaton, Ill.: Tyndale, 1989.

An excellent encyclopedia of Lewis quotes, some of them quite lengthy.

Sayer, George, and Lyle W. Dorsett. *Jack: A Life of C. S. Lewis.* Wheaton, Ill.: Crossway, 2005.

A biography from one of Lewis's students, who knew him for 20 years.

Other Fiction Books by C. S. Lewis

Pilgrim's Regress (1933). Grand Rapids, MI: Eerdmans, 1992.

Lewis's first book published after he became a Christian. An allegory that plays off *Pilgrim's Progress*, with many obscure allusions and references, and thus difficult to read for many. We both like it, however, and would recommend it, but not as the first Lewis book you read.

The Screwtape Letters (1942; revised edition, including "Screwtape Proposes a Toast," 1982). New York: Macmillan, 1982.

> Fictional letters from a "senior devil" to his young apprentice nephew on how to tempt his human subject. A favorite of many, but not of Lewis himself.

Out of the Silent Planet (1938). New York: Macmillan, 1965.

Perelandra (1943). New York: Macmillan, 1965.

That Hideous Strength (1945). New York: Macmillan, 1965.

> If you like science fiction or imaginative books, you may really like Lewis's Space Trilogy. *Perelandra* was one of Lewis's own favorites—and one of mine (Cheryl). *That Hideous Strength* is dense and philosophical; start with one of the other two.

The Great Divorce (1946). New York: Macmillan, 1946.

> An imaginary bus trip from hell to heaven, which is pictured figuratively. We see only the edges of this imaginary heaven, where people lose their selfishness if they decide to stay. Many choose instead to return to hell, where they can keep their selfish ways.

Till We Have Faces (1956). San Diego: Harcourt Brace Jovanovitch, 1956.

> Lewis's last fiction work, deemed by him and many others to be his best. Based on the myth of Psyche and Cupid, with many additions by Lewis.

Boxen: The Imaginary World of the Young C. S. Lewis (1985).

> Edited by Walter Hooper, this is a collection of animal stories that were also illustrated by Lewis as a young child. They are a precursor to Narnia.

Important Nonfiction Books by C. S. Lewis

Mere Christianity (1943). New York: Macmillan, 1943.

His perennial multimillion best-selling apology for the Christian faith. Perhaps the best simple explanation of Christianity for today's reader.

The Problem of Pain (1940). New York: Macmillan, 1962.

Lewis deals with the mystery of suffering and how God uses it for our good.

The Abolition of Man (1943). New York: Macmillan, 1988.

A discussion of how and why objective truth has been eliminated from public discourse and how that affects our being human.

Letter to Malcolm: Chiefly on Prayer (1964). San Diego: Harcourt Brace & Company, 1964.

This book deals with all the key aspects of prayer in the life of the Christian.

"Reflections on the Psalms" (1958). In *The Inspirational Writings of C. S. Lewis*. New York: Inspirational Press, 1994.

A look at this special genre within Scripture in which we communicate all our hopes, joys, fears, and disappointments to God.

God in the Dock: Essays on Theology and Ethics (1970). Grand Rapids, MI: Eerdmans, 1970.

A collection of the best of his essays related to the spiritual issues of his time.

The Business of Heaven: Daily Readings from C. S. Lewis (1984).

Edited by Walter Hooper, this book provides an excellent devotional collection of his spiritual works.

Good Websites and Other Nonprint Resources

http://cslewis.drzeus.net   Into the Wardrobe: an excellent resource for Narnia research, including numerous articles on Lewis and Narnia.

http://disney.go.com/disneypictures/narnia/   A movie-based website, for those who want to know more about the movie.

www.thenarniaacademy.org/menu.php   Another thorough, relatively comprehensive website on all things Narnia.

www.calormen.com/Calormen/encyclopedia.htm   A Narnian encyclopedia, defining Narnian places and creatures.

The Chronicles of Narnia Radio Theatre   CD dramatizations of all seven volumes, available in a set of 19 CDs from Focus on the Family. Hosted and introduced by Douglas Gresham, Lewis's stepson.

Index